WHAT PEOPLE ARE SAYING ABOUT *COMMUNICATION IQ* AND FRED AND ANNA KENDALL

The 7 Life Languages communication profile has been one of the most powerful and effective teaching and training tools that I have had the pleasure of using. Since most of our interactive behavior involves communicating with others, the knowledge gained from learning about ourselves and others through the Life Languages can only enhance, heal, strengthen, and improve our personal and professional relationships. This powerful tool can be used in any setting. The wisdom gained when individuals learn their own unique set of Life Languages is enlightening and automatically helps to create a greater appreciation for diverse perspectives. This powerful information has been a significant addition to the curriculum in our Management and Business Administration Program.

—*Linda Morable*, Ph.D.
Professor of management, Richland College, Dallas, TX

I have attended many seminars on communication, personal growth, and team-building. The 7 Life Languages seminar was outstanding—the best! I gained new insights into myself, my family, and other members of my team. The entire staff enjoyed the seminar, too. We laughed and we learned. We saw each other in a different light. We defined strengths and goals of our entire team. More importantly, we all returned to our workplace and our personal lives with renewed energy and fresh insights into our relationships and ourselves.

—*Sandi Hammons*
Founder, American Institute of Intradermal Cosmetics, Inc.
Arlington, TX

Young Truck Sales began working with Carolyn Santos in learning the 7 Life Languages with our Executive management team. It was truly an awakening to learn how each of us naturally communicated and how those styles had actually created tension and misunderstandings between our close, six-person team. Learning and understanding how each of us communicated enables us to not only understand our differences, but appreciate them and begin to truly utilize each other's strengths and recognize when we were going down the miscommunication rabbit hole and stop it! We later brought the entire management team into the Life Languages program and we have enjoyed similar results. It is a transformative process and we will be taking the next steps in Life Languages soon for our executive team. I have found that close to 100 percent of problems we have, whether internally or with clients, stem from poor communication. Learning the 7 Life Languages has peeled back the mystery and given us real tools to understand ourselves, our teams, and our clients to enable us to reduce the crises and stress that arise from poor communication.

—*Craig A. Young*
President, Young Trucks, Canton, OH

I have utilized the Kendall Life Languages Profile in my professional work in human resources for several years. As many in my profession are aware, successful companies are those organizations where employee engagement is high. Effective communication is a key driver of employee engagement. As we onboard employees to our organization, we emphasize that good communication is the responsibility of all employees. It is one of our core values. All new employees take the Kendall Life Languages Profile. It provides them with insight into their own communication preferences and provides them with information to assimilate and work effectively with their team members. It is also a great tool to understand and remedy conflict within work groups. In addition, when employee performance issues arise, it serves as a reference to help the manager understand how to effectively approach these discussions with the employee. The KLLP is a system that addresses all aspects of the employee life-cycle and is the most effective and comprehensive communication system on the market today.

—*Leslie Horwitz*, MBA, SHRM-SCP
Former Global HR Programs Leader
ECOM Agroindustrial Corp. Ltd.

I am pleased to recommend the Kendall Life Languages Profile instrument (KLLP). I have found it to be a very accurate assessment tool, as well as an indispensable day-to-day communication and consensus building aid. I have spent over twenty years in the food service business. I have functioned as the president of Wendy's Restaurants of Canada, an executive vice president of Brice Foods, president of I Can't Believe It's Yogurt US Operations, and owner/operator of eighteen Wendy's Old Fashioned Hamburger Restaurants. During all of these postings, I have had exposure to many management skill profile instruments, but none have proven to be as valuable as the KLLP instrument. I urge any organization that is looking to more fully understand the dynamics between employees, departments, and project teams to give serious consideration to using the KLLP process.

—*Mark R. Liebel*
Vice president, Business Development, Dippin Dots, Inc.

The two presentations you have made at our company were excellent. It amazes me how accurate your profile results have been. We are beginning to grasp the increasing implications of a staff who understand more about communicating with fellow employees who are operating from completely different motivations. It has increased our awareness of each other and our individual ways of dealing with the situations we face as we work together. It is my intent to have the 100+ employees of this company participate in the program. The company is currently working to integrate your LLI program into our daily work programming and training.

—*Mitch Clark*
Founder, TOMCAT Global, Inc.

Healthy relationships are key to every business and family. My husband, Marcus, and I decided to implement the concept of the Life Languages years ago and found that it is a wonderful tool of communication, not only corporately at Daystar Television Network, but within our own family. Fred and Anna Kendall are dear friends and their sincerity in developing and empowering people with character-based-communication surpasses the ordinary tactics currently used in the corporate world. I know *Communication IQ* will be life-changing and we highly recommend it!

—*Joni Lamb*
Co-founder, Daystar Television Network

I want to compliment Life Languages International on developing an instrument that is so understandable and accurate. The 7 Life Languages communication profile is the most accurate and user-friendly I have seen. The profile is so detailed and clear, it will enlighten and give insights to anyone willing to use it. The Life Languages program has impacted my own life more than anything I have come in contact with other than the Bible. This is quite extraordinary! The training seminar I attended was thorough and extremely practical. The coaches were incredible and real. Thank you for developing such a great tool/resource. I will be able to use this in both my personal and professional life.

—*Phyllis Fitzwater*
Adult critical care chaplain, Orlando Regional Healthcare System, FL

I have known Fred and Anna Kendall for over thirty years during which time I've had ample opportunity to read their books and use their program. As the former CEO of four multi-million-dollar organizations and the current CEO of the Union Gospel Mission of Sioux Falls, South Dakota, I've relied upon the 7 Life Languages program and the Kendalls' consulting, counseling, and instruction for building a successful executive team in every situation. Each time we've hired them to conduct seminars for our staff members, they far exceeded our expectations. Thanks to their expertise and excellent communication skills, my staff have grown closer and more productive. They have learned how to communicate more successfully with one another and how to avoid the pitfalls that hinder the growth in their spirit of unity. Any organization that needs and wants more efficiency, production, and cooperation among their employees should avail themselves of the Kendalls' expertise and willingness to help. They and their staff are very talented, knowledgeable in the area of interpersonal communication, and a blessing to all who are looking to improve their spirit of cooperation.

—*Ron Gonzales*
CEO, Union Gospel Mission, Sioux Falls, SD

I want to personally say how pleased we are with the 7 Life Languages communication profile and training presented to the uniformed and non-uniformed employees. For entirely too long, communication problems or hindrances have taken a toll in law enforcement, business, individuals, families, and interactive situations. The 7 Life Languages program is the most positive step anyone can take to improve on this age-old problem of communication. Life Languages promotes an atmosphere conducive to wanting to learn how to communicate more effectively. Since we need to communicate with others on a daily basis, I cannot recommend a better program aimed at the personal success of self, others, and the organization.

—Lt. Tim Rich
Sheriff's Department, Denton County, TX

I applaud you for the incredibly accurate instrument you have developed. It is not only accurate, but you include with it the most usable and understandable information that I have seen with any other assessment tool. The other counselors in our practice feel the same confidence in the instrument. The people with whom we have used it have been enlightened about why they act the way they do, and have been set free to be themselves. The couples with whom we have used it (more than 150 and counting) have discovered a new appreciation for and understanding of each other. They also say that it has greatly improved their ability to communicate and accomplish tasks together.

—H. LeRoy Arnold Jr., Ph.D.
President, Keys to Life Ministries & Counseling Centers
Titusville, FL

It is my pleasure to commend you for the impressive effort you made in the effective communication presentations. It is clearly evident that the communication patterns of the more than 280 employees who participated in the program are changing for the better.

—*M. Jane Dailey*, MS, RN, CHE
Vice president, Nursing Services, Aroostook Medical Center
Presque Isle, ME

As the president and CEO of a fast-growing, renewable energy company, the Life Languages program has been invaluable. The culture at miEnergy is paramount to our achieving our vision and communication plays a vital role in that process. My experience with coach Scott Epp has been empowering and transformational. Scott first equipped me to understand and share the Life Languages material and then facilitated sessions with our team. Through these sessions, each individual grew not only in their understanding of themselves but also in their appreciation for others. The Life Languages exercise has allowed us to support our vision even better through deeper relationships and productive communication. This tool can not only assist within a corporate culture but in every personal relationship in life. It has been a positive investment and we are continuing to integrate Scott and the Life Languages tool into our training and development.

—*Kevin Bergeron*
President and CEO, miEnergy, Saskatoon, Saskatchewan, Canada

Life Languages was invited to present to our management and sales team at Trinity Title of Texas. Jerry Parsons was the presenter and gave great insight that was beneficial to our team collectively as well as individually. The seminar was outstanding in providing the team with personal applications that will improve their interactions with each other and in their chosen sphere of influence. I highly recommend this company for any group or organization that desires to better relate to individuals and attain positive results for greater success.

—*Cheryl A. Finney*
DFW Division President, Trinity Title of Texas

Property Damage Appraisers (PDA) is a dynamic company woven together with diverse people contributing an array of communication styles. Life Languages has empowered PDA to embrace and accept our similarities and differences and to leverage these traits to our advantage in our business as well as our personal lives. Our respective Life Languages profiles, ongoing training, and enculturation of Life Languages tenets have dramatically increased our awareness of how we communicate in various situations, equipping us with strategies to employ while communicating with others. The benefits have been, and continue to be, obvious and tangible and are being adopted as a company-wide initiative.

—*Tom Dolfay*
President/CEO, Property Damage Appraisers, Inc.

COMMUNICATION
IQ

A PROVEN WAY TO *INFLUENCE, LEAD,* AND *MOTIVATE* PEOPLE

FRED & ANNA KENDALL

WHITAKER
HOUSE

Communication IQ
A Proven Way to Influence, Lead, and Motivate People

Life Languages International
2711 Valley View Lane, Suite 103
Dallas, TX 75234
www.lifelanguages.com

ISBN: 978-1-64123-209-8
eBook ISBN: 978-1-64123-210-4
Printed in the United States of America

Whitaker House
1030 Hunt Valley Circle
New Kensington, PA 15068
www.whitakerhouse.com

Library of Congress Cataloging-in-Publication Data
Names: Kendall, Fred, 1937- author. | Kendall, Anna.
Title: Communication IQ : a proven way to influence, lead, and motivate
  people / Fred Kendall, Anna Kendall.
Description: New kensington, PA : Whitaker House, 2019. | Series: Life
  languages |
Identifiers: LCCN 2018052835 (print) | LCCN 2018058832 (ebook) | ISBN
  9781641232104 (e-book) | ISBN 9781641232098 (hardback) |
Subjects: LCSH: Business communication. | Leadership—Psychological aspects.
  | BISAC: BUSINESS & ECONOMICS / Business Communication / General. |
  BUSINESS & ECONOMICS / Leadership.
Classification: LCC HF5718 (ebook) | LCC HF5718 .K456 2019 (print) | DDC
  658.4/5—dc23
LC record available at https://lccn.loc.gov/2018052835

1 2 3 4 5 6 7 8 9 10 11 **LIJ** 26 25 24 23 22 21 20 19

DEDICATION

My wife, Anna, has been working beside me over the past thirty years as we have discovered, developed, and refined the 7 Life Languages as well as our character-based communication tool, the Kendall Life Languages Profile (KLLP). Anna has been my tireless partner in writing this book. She is gifted with profound wisdom, knowledge, and creativity. Her thoughts and insights are found throughout the book.

We would both like to dedicate this book to those who have helped us make it happen: our five hundred certified coaches around the world, all of whom have worked, encouraged, tested, and proven the 7 Life Languages system of communication. Thank you for introducing the 7 Life Languages worldwide to the many thousands who have embraced our concept and given testimony to the changed lives and strengthened corporate cultures that have resulted.

—*Fred Kendall*

CONTENTS

FOREWORD

Fred and Anna Kendall have spent years studying, defining, proving, and improving methods of successful communication. I am honored to be the Chief Operating Officer of their creation, Life Languages International.

Having known Fred and Anna both professionally and personally for over thirty years, it has been exciting and rewarding to see their idea become a reality that continues to change so many lives.

During Fred's college years, his degrees in psychology emphasized leadership, tactics, and strategy. Then as a U.S. Marine Corps captain and successful entrepreneur, his interests gravitated toward understanding and helping people develop positive character and effective communication skills.

Anna's background in radio, television, and public speaking took them into many fields of endeavor, including joint ownership of psychiatric hospital programs in Dallas/Fort Worth, Texas, Albuquerque, New Mexico, and Newport Beach, California, as well as multiple psychiatric and psychological outpatient clinics.

With the collaboration of psychiatrists, psychologists, social workers, nurses, therapists, and other professionals, the Kendalls created, tested, and proved the success of their concept: the communication styles of the 7 Life Languages. Their character-based communication tool has grown and evolved to become the amazingly accurate Kendall Life Languages Profile (KLLP), which is uniquely diagnostic, prescriptive, and life-changing.

The 7 Life Languages and the KLLP have been used by thousands of individuals, couples, families, businesses, corporations, and government agencies. The program has been taught at colleges and universities. Thanks to our international network of coaches, it's currently being used in more than 185 countries.

It is the Kendalls' hope that this book will enrich your life by helping you discover the different communication styles that we all possess.

If you'd like to take a personal Life Languages Profile at any time, you'll find instructions for a free, abbreviated version, as well as the full profile, at the end of this book.

—*Gerald Parsons*, COO
Life Languages International
Dallas, TX

ACKNOWLEDGMENTS

Thanks to the many people who have helped us with the development of the 7 Life Languages concept, the Kendall Life Languages Profile (KLLP), and the writing and development of this book.

To Marcus and Joni Lamb, their family, and the staff of the Daystar Television Network, who immediately saw the value of the KLLP years ago and have literally proclaimed the benefits around the world.

To Carolyn Santos, our international training director, who has lived the 7 Life Languages for the last twenty years as she has traveled throughout the world to reach and train others.

To our corporate chief operating officer, Gerald Parsons, who has been a tireless encouragement to us, as well as a navigating force for the steady growth of Life Languages International.

To our LLI Office Manager, Anne Schultz, who has kept the corporate wheels of progress running!

To Phil and Betty Klein, who graciously gave of their time and talents to edit and improve the first complete draft of this manuscript. Their insight and creativity are greatly appreciated.

To Kevin Badinger, our information technology expert, who has shepherded us through multiple software versions and improvements of the KLLP.

To Shaun and Tina Naidoo, who adopted us into their family and have been a part of major corporate decisions, growth, and development of the Life Languages.

To the hundreds of Certified Life Languages Communication Coaches, without whom we would still be trying to spread this message alone. Thank you for joining us in making the Life Languages known around the world.

And to the businesses, organizations, clients, friends, and family who have walked this journey with us. Our heartfelt thanks to each of you.

PART ONE:

OVERVIEW

1

A UNIVERSAL NEED

Imagine trying to communicate with every person in the world—more than seven and a half billion people. That's a daunting idea, isn't it? Now suppose you only had to communicate with seven people. Not so tough, right?

The fact is, if you can communicate with those seven people, you can communicate with everyone else. Because we all speak the 7 Life Languages.

Unlike English, Mandarin Chinese, Spanish, or any of the world's six thousand spoken languages, the 7 Life Languages are communication styles. They are dynamic, definable, character-based, and universally successful for both professional and personal relationships.

The great news is, you already speak all seven of these languages to some degree of fluency and skill. As you learn to recognize them, you will be able to communicate effectively with people in every situation, from all walks of life.

FASTER ISN'T ALWAYS BETTER

Since we entered the twenty-first century, there has been a definite change in the *way* people communicate and a bigger change in *how* we relate to one another. The Internet and cell phones give us access to instant, one-on-one communication across the globe, as well as the ability to interact anywhere, at any time. But this has not necessarily led to better understanding and improved interactions. As technology continues to improve, almost on a daily basis, our *standards of communication* have fallen, nearly to the point of being overlooked.

Are two teenagers sending a series of emojis back and forth to each other truly communicating on a deeply personal, intellectual level? What about the young, new manager who sends a long-time salesperson a text that reads, "Btw, u subt. Smh. 4col, cya nxt k?"[1]

Good communication skills are particularly imperative for managers and leaders. They also improve our relationships with family, friends, coworkers, and everyone else we meet.

Marriage counselors say the number one reason that marriages fail is a communication problem. If a couple can communicate, they can deal with every issue they may face, whether it be financial disagreements, parenting troubles, contentious in-laws, or anything else.

---

1. "By the way, you screwed up big time. Shaking my head. For crying out loud, cover your a– next time, okay?"

For us to live and work together harmoniously, we need to understand each other. It's possible to do so if you learn the 7 Life Languages. We believe they will provide you with a revolutionary way to act, think, and feel about communication.

COMMUNICATE OR DIE

Capt. Eugene "Red" McDaniel, a Navy pilot, was shot down in North Vietnam and held as a prisoner of war for six years. In his book, *Scars and Stripes,* he described the desperate need for prisoners to communicate with one another to maintain morale.[2]

On many occasions, McDaniel and his fellow POWs endured torture rather than give up their attempts to stay in touch with each other. When he was in solitary confinement, his fellow POWs risked death by working out a complicated communication system that included writing messages under their plates, coughing, using slang, tapping out code on their cell walls, laughing, scratching, and even spitting or flapping laundry a certain number of times to transmit letters of the alphabet.

"One thing I knew was that I had to have communication with my own people," said McDaniel. "Like me, they wanted to live through their imprisonment."

Any lone, isolated POW would feel weak and helpless. Communicating with each other gave them the strength to go on.

---

2. Eugene Red McDaniel, *Scars and Stripes: The True Story of One Man's Courage Facing Death as a POW in Vietnam* (Washington, DC: WND Books, 2012)

For those brave men, it was communicate or die. And for personal and corporate relationships, it is communicate or watch your career or relationships die a cruel death—the death of disconnectedness, neglect, or misunderstanding, or the stone-silent death of apathy. Often, it is not just your career that dies. Sometimes, even the corporation dies if communication is not a priority.   —Anna Kendall

2

COMMUNICATION INTELLIGENCES

Peter Drucker, often called the father of American management, claimed that 80 percent of all management problems are a result of faulty communication.

Good communication doesn't just happen. For most people, it's a skill learned over time.

Before we discovered and developed the 7 Life Languages, Anna and I used to think we were good communicators. We were both articulate and comfortable talking to other people. We could carry on a conversation with anyone. But being good at talking doesn't mean you're a good communicator. Sometimes, our communication faltered, especially between the two of us. We didn't understand what the other said or meant.

> We tend to judge what we don't understand.
> —Carolyn Santos
> Life Languages' International Director of Training

WHAT IS COMMUNICATION?

Communication is the process of transmitting information from one person to another or a group to create a shared understanding and feeling. The word "communication" comes from the Latin word *communicare*, meaning to "share or experience common union."

People who are communicating are not necessarily agreeing with each other. Instead, they are transmitting information in the hopes that it is understood and received as intended.

Have you ever felt like you and your boss, coworker, or assistant were not communicating? Like you are speaking a different cultural language? That no matter what you say or do, it's taken the wrong way or *they* "fail to understand" your point or message?

Do you know someone whose actions or words often come across as an insult or a putdown? Someone who always seems impatient or in a bad mood?

Imagine how peaceful and productive it would be if you were working in an environment where *you* are understood and you also understand *everyone else*. It would be like having a real-time interpreter at your side, explaining everything that was said or done, with detail and clarity.

FRED'S OBSERVATIONS AS A MARINE

I have always been a student of human nature. While I was in the Marine Corps, I began to observe the different initial reaction of the troop members to one another, as well as how the group, as a whole, reacted to orders given to them by their senior officers.

One group seemed to want to *always stay busy*. Individuals who were "all talk and no action" bothered them. This group wanted to go out and make things happen. Interestingly, this group was further subdivided into two similar but different groups: those who wanted to stay active and busy, no matter where the assigned location was, and those who didn't need to go off somewhere to be active. They just wanted to be busy. Activity was definitely a part of their reaction to life. Many of these Marines, during a wartime situation, seemed to want to go into action or combat almost before the "order to move out" was even issued. Before these Marines even had time to think or feel, they were already moving out!

A second group consisted of troops who were *acceptance friendly* toward a given plan presented by their superior officer. They would tend to show more care and concern about their fellow Marines than the contents of the just-presented military plan. This group was led by their feelings. They were expressive and usually energized by their passions or emotions. These individuals would bring emotional cohesiveness to a group. If one of them got a "dear John letter" or similar bad news from home, they had a much more difficult time of accepting the information emotionally.

The third group were those who *were led by their thoughts* when the troops were given direct orders or plans. If possible, when the situation allowed, many of the individuals in this group would ask questions and want to know more data or facts. Then they would consider, think, and try to better understand the nature or goal of the plan.

I enjoyed my time in the Marine Corps and later, when I was in the business world, I realized how outstanding the leadership training was in the USMC.

As we started trying to understand interactive communication, three types of intelligences or categories of people came to mind. There are individuals who:

1. Act first

2. Feel first

3. Think first

After thousands of hours of research and discussion, we started to identify these behaviors in people we knew, met, or read about. Years of observation and study gave us an extensive list of subdivided differences in these three life categories: kinetic/action; emotive/feeling; and cognitive/thinking.

We have come to understand these categories as different intelligences. Each of the three have strong, healthy descriptions and each can have some unproductive results when carried to extreme or subjected to stress that becomes distress.

During our years of owning and managing three psychiatric hospital programs, we discussed this theory with professionals on our staff. They came to agree that these three categories could also be described as three types of intelligences. As we look at these three intelligences and the 7 Life Languages, remember that any combination can be very effective for business or corporate leaders. Each Life Language simply leads differently.

This chart shows the three communication intelligence groupings and seven life languages:

COMMUNICATION INTELLIGENCE GROUPS		
Kinetic/Action	Emotive/Feeling	Cognitive/Thinking
Mover	Influencer	Shaper
Doer	Responder	Producer
		Contemplator

All of us communicate in all three categories. We all act, feel, and think.

1. **Kinetic/Action Intelligence.** Before people with this intelligence stop to think or consider their feelings, they very easily move into action of some sort. There are two communication styles or Life Languages that come under this category: Mover and Doer. Those having one of these Life Languages as their preferred communication style are usually in motion with *instinctive* intelligence or *practical* intelligence.

2. **Emotive/Feeling Intelligence.** Those speaking the Life Languages from the emotive intelligence tend to be relational and their first response to life, people, or situations is through

their feelings, which they reveal through their speech or behavior. They subconsciously respond with their emotive awareness or intelligence. This category is made up of two Life Languages with varying degrees of *relational* intelligence: Influencer and Responder.

3. Cognitive/Thinking Intelligence. The first response speakers of the cognitive/thinking intelligence have to life, others, or situations is to think. Some think rapidly, while some may spend more time reasoning, gathering facts, considering, pondering, and evaluating, but all of them think first. They subconsciously respond with their cognitive awareness or *analytical* intelligence. The three Life Languages in this category are: Shaper, Producer, and Contemplator.

All of us often go through these three intelligence categories rapidly and subconsciously. However, it's important to know and understand the *order* in which this occurs. This "intelligence awareness" gives us a greater understanding of ourselves and others.

For example, if your first intelligence is kinetic and you want to communicate with someone whose first intelligence is cognitive, you will realize that you must stop, listen, and think with them before taking action.

3

THE KENDALL LIFE LANGUAGES PROFILE (KLLP)

T here's been a quiet revolution going on in the field of corporate communication.

Managers want to understand their staffs. Executives want everyone to be happy and productive. Employees want to feel valued and more at ease with their coworkers.

We were driven to write this book to help people accomplish all of this—and more.

There's one point we want to stress before we delve into the 7 Life Languages. No Life Languages communication style is better than another. You're not going to take the Life

Languages Assessment and think to yourself, "No wonder I can't get people to agree with me." No! Instead, you'll be thinking, "Wow, now everything is beginning to make sense!"

> Your personal Life Languages Assessment shows your communication style, written in a *positive way* so you'll gladly share it with others. You and your coworkers or friends will find it enjoyable as well as enlightening.
> —Anna Kendall

Over the past twenty-five years, approximately 225,000 people have taken the Kendall Life Languages Profile (KLLP) assessment program. It's been used by individuals, couples, families, businesses, universities, governments, churches, and other organizations around the world. The KLLP has been subjected to enormous technical, vocational, and market research analyses. While most testing instruments measure aptitude, personality, mental health, job skills, and the like, the KLLP uniquely measures your personal communication style and helps you learn to "speak" all 7 Life Languages fluently and effectively.

We have written this book and developed the Life Languages Assessment to introduce more people to the concept of *Communication IQ* and, we hope, inspire them to learn their KLLP. The profile exposes the unique ways that you communicate, your preferred methods of communication, and your areas of unique effectiveness.

Everyone speaks the 7 Life Languages and all combinations of these communication styles are great. All have strong, positive character qualities. There is no Life Language that cannot relate to another, although some may take a little more effort.

The following charts give examples of information gleaned from one person's Kendall Life Languages Profile, starting with their primary or most active communication style.

Communication Preference	Language	Language Intensity	Rating	Gap
Primary	SHAPER	82.93	High	0
Second	INFLUENCER	62.69	Moderate	20.23
Third	MOVER	52.58	Moderate	10.12
Fourth	RESPONDER	42.46	Moderate	10.12
Fifth	PRODUCER	41.96	Moderate	0.51
Sixth	DOER	41.45	Moderate	0.51
Seventh	CONTEMPLATOR	22.23	Low	19.22
Range				60.69
Overall Intensity		71.82	High	

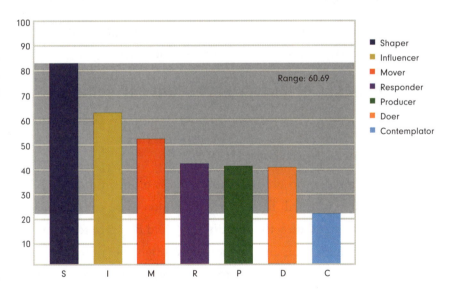

KENDALL LIFE LANGUAGES PROFILE (EXAMPLE)

The top chart shows this person's first and primary Life Language is Shaper; he identified with 83 percent of the Shaper characteristics. His second and third languages, respectively, are Influencer (62 percent) and Mover (52 percent). This person can easily and naturally speak all three of these languages and go back and forth between them. It will likely be easy for this person to communicate with other people who speak Shaper, Influencer, or Mover as their preferred Life Languages.

Next are three moderate Life Languages in the 40 percent range, which this person can reach by choice and without too much effort. He would not necessarily stay in those communication styles for too long because doing so may be stressful or require too much effort. However, he can use one of those languages to communicate with those who have Responder, Producer, or Doer as their preferred communication styles.

People who speak high Contemplator might be a challenge for this person, unless he studied the 7 Life Languages.

OVERALL INTENSITY LEVEL AND GAP SCORES

The overall intensity level score reveals the strength, energy, and passion any person displays when they are communicating. The higher the score, the higher the individual's drive to communicate. High overall intensity is often an indication of someone who will fight for their opinion to be considered, exercise control (directly or indirectly), and do more to maintain communication and relationships. High overall intensity persons may draw attention to themselves and may be more prone to conflict.

Lower overall intensity scores indicate those who generally do not compete to be heard, although they may have valuable contributions to make. Unfortunately, these people are sometimes overlooked or ignored.

Regardless of whether a person has a high, moderate, or low overall intensity, this score doesn't measure whether they have passion, but how or if we will experience that intensity when in meetings or working together on a project.

The "Gap" score in the first chart measures the distance between two Life Languages. The greater the gap, the more effort it takes to move from one Life Language to the other. The smaller the gap, the easier it is to move between the two.

Indicator	Score	Result
1. Acceptance Level	98	High
2. Interactive Style Extrovert	37	Moderate
3. Internal Control	29	Low
4. Intrusion Level	43	Moderate
5. Projective Level	85	High
6. Susceptibility to Stress	11	Low
7. Learning Preference Order		
Visual	56	High
Physical	38	Moderate
Auditory	6	Low

COMMUNICATION INDICATORS CHART

The last chart offers further insights into a person's communication style. Among other indicators, it measures:

+ Acceptance level—how you tend to view yourself

+ Interactive style—whether you prefer working alone or in groups

+ Internal control level—self-disciplined vs. impulsive

- ♦ Intrusion level—how you handle interruptions or distractions

- ♦ Projective indicator—how important others' perceptions and opinions are to you

The online Life Languages Assessment tool that we provide for *Communication IQ* readers will simply indicate your primary Life Language. If you undertake the complete Kendall Life Languages Profile, you will receive a thorough report on your communication preferences, with charts like the ones we've shown here as well as explanations that will increase your self-awareness and suggestions on ways to be more effective in your professional and personal interactions.

SEPARATE COMMUNICATION STYLES

The 7 Life Languages don't merge or mingle. Each one stands alone because they are separate communication styles. You automatically move from one to another as you seek a path to communicate effectively.

Knowing your preferred methods of communication and your levels of intensity for them will give you a lot of information about who you are. Knowing this about others will help you to understand and relate to them more effectively. Your KLLP may confirm things you already knew about yourself or you may be surprised by the results.

We can all learn to recognize the language another is speaking and go to that communication style by choice, even if it's our last one. There could be key employees in your team, department, or company who speak your sixth or seventh Life Languages. Without learning to understand or communicate with them, you could be setting yourself up for failure or even lose good people due to miscommunication and misunderstanding.

SPEAKING WITH AN ACCENT

Whatever your first Life Language is, you will speak all the others with the *accent* of the first one, just as we do with cultural languages. If your first language is English and you also speak Spanish, it's very probable that you speak Spanish with an English accent. If you then learn to speak Russian, you will do so with an English accent, not Spanish.

This is also true with Life Languages. In the KLLP example we've provided, you see the individual's first Life Language is a Shaper, the second is Influencer, and so on. Thus, this person will "speak" all seven Life Languages with a Shaper accent.

LIVING THE DREAM?

Too often, young men and women attempt to fulfill the dreams their parents have for them, such as entering the same field as Mom or Dad or joining a family business. They soon discover that they are unhappy, unfulfilled, and living in distress and depression.

Sometimes, a person has been in a career for twenty years and is still not sure what they want to do with their life. This is not unusual. All that person knows is that they feel stuck, trapped, and defeated, living in a state of emotional hopelessness about their future, both personally and professionally. Happiness and fulfillment seem to be beyond their reach.

Why? Most likely, they are in careers that do not fit their gifts, desires, or passions. They may not even know what these are. But they can receive tremendous, in-depth insights from the Kendall Life Languages Profile.

> When an individual's occupation lines up with their Life Languages profile, we almost always hear those people saying things like, "I would enjoy doing this job *even* if I weren't paid!" Or "I'm doing what I love. Why should I retire?" Unfortunately, for many, that "dream job" seems to be always just beyond reach. But it needn't be. —Anna Kendall

By learning your personal Life Languages profile, plus understanding all seven communication styles, you will find that conflicts and misunderstandings are decreased and often even eliminated. Plus, it may be an exciting adventure to find a new career that suits your talents and dreams.

BOTH DIAGNOSTIC AND PRESCRIPTIVE

The Kendall Life Languages Profile is both diagnostic and prescriptive. It diagnoses your strengths, passions, and even possible weaknesses. You will gain an almost immediate self-awareness and understanding of yourself, learning why you react in certain ways, both at work and in your personal life. And as you contemplate the 7 Life Languages, you will come to realize when you are switching from one communication style to another.

KLLP is prescriptive in that your newfound information will give you insights about others so you can adjust your communication style and connect with them successfully and effectively.

Other testing instruments tell you about yourself, but not what to do with that information or how to communicate. The KLLP teaches you to be self-aware, internalize the information about the seven communication styles, and reach others by speaking their language.

THE 7 LIFE LANGUAGES

The seven chapters in the next section cover the 7 Life Languages. For brevity's sake, we say "a Mover," "a Responder," and the like, but *we are only doing so in order to talk about a single communication style.* There are no "pure" speakers of only one Life Language.

Each chapter includes:

LIFE LANGUAGE ICON AND EXPLANATION

Our initial icons for the Life Languages were very detailed and we wanted to share our thought processes behind them. We have since created simplified versions that express the language's overall tone.

SYMBOL FROM NATURE

The lives of different animals give us a whimsical way to examine each language.

COLOR

We look at the colors that each communication style may evoke.

POSITIVE CHARACTERISTICS

Charts detail some of the outstanding qualities of each Life Language.

FOUR KEYS TO SUCCESSFUL COMMUNICATION

1. **Answer their filter question**: Each Life Language has an invisible filter that colors and affects how the person receives incoming and outgoing communication. Like wearing a pair of tinted glasses, this filter gives us a silent, subconscious message that instantly asks a question. Studying the various filters of all 7 Life Languages helps us to understand just how deeply imbedded our perceptions are. We see and define the world through our filter question.

2. **Meet their need from others**: All of us have needs that, when met, cause us to feel appreciated, motivated, and understood.

3. **Encourage their passion**: We are all hard-wired with a passion for different accomplishments. Knowing this can help us in our efforts to order our lives and relationships accordingly.

4. **Validate their character:** All the Life Languages have multiple characteristics, but each has one key character quality that stands out, defines their communication style, and appreciates validation from others.

ESSENTIAL TRAIT TO CULTIVATE

This is the one trait that you may need to develop, depending on your key Life Languages.

SUCCESS HABIT TO DEVELOP

What key habit must be developed in order to achieve success? This is a habit not naturally in the DNA of each Life

Language that must be intentionally practiced until it begins to come naturally.

DISTRESS FLARES

You sometimes see distress flares along the highway beside a car that's broken down or has a flat tire. The flares alert other drivers to prevent collisions with the disabled vehicle, or signal that someone needs help.

When any of the 7 Life Languages become stressed or distressed, each tends to send recognizable signals or flares— warning signs that let others know something isn't right. These distress flares are ways we begin to sabotage our personal and professional lives in very predictable ways. Fortunately, if we are aware of them, they can be easily resolved.

If we have developed a good sense of self-awareness, we can catch ourselves as we are sending these signals and take steps to alleviate the problem. If we fail to make that choice, we can be less successful in our relationships and career.

> We may express our distress flares in our second or even our third Life Language. It is important to be aware of all the different ones and be able to identify which flares we tend to operate in when under stress.
>
> —Carolyn Santos
> Life Languages international training director

Remember, we have choices. We can decide to take responsibility for our negative behavior and choose to be happy, healthy, and successful. We can even choose to deal with negative issues in positive ways. The Life Languages reveal more choices than we ever knew we had.

Once we recognize the ways we each handle *distress*, we can bring ourselves out of this behavior by choice, or others nearby can recognize the symptoms of distress and look at our profile to determine how to help.

People change when the pain of staying the same is greater than the pain of changing.   —Anna Kendall

LEADERSHIP STYLES

All seven communication styles can make successful, effective leaders.

PROFESSIONS, CLUES, AND EXAMPLES

Each chapter on the 7 Life Languages also examines possible professions, provides clues for communicating with each language, and offers examples of well-known people who did— or do—seem to communicate overwhelmingly in that style.

It's important to note that no matter what your Life Languages results, you are a unique, special individual with many gifts and talents that the world needs. Celebrate who you are!

If you have any questions, email Life Languages International at info@lifelanguages.com or call 972-406-1313 to schedule a consultation with a Life Languages certified coach.

PART TWO:

THE 7 LIFE LANGUAGES

PRIMARY LIFE LANGUAGES BY POPULATION

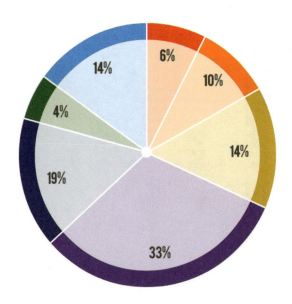

Approximate percentages of population with these as their primary Life Languages:

- Mover: 6 percent
- Doer: 10 percent
- Influencer: 14 percent
- Responder: 33 percent
- Shaper: 19 percent
- Producer: 4 percent
- Contemplator: 14 percent

4

MOVER:
THINKING OUTSIDE THE BOX

THE MOVER ICON

The original Mover icon features a flying standard with the image of a light bulb, a bugle, and a small hand holding a hammer, signifying the action/kinetic intelligence. The new icon retains the flag because Movers are known as standard-bearers. Wherever they go, they want to raise standards of behavior or performance. They lead the charge and jump into action.

The icon has the Mover name written as though it's in motion because Movers seldom stay still. They prefer to be on the go.

Movers are also full of creative ideas as well as fresh ways of doing old things. They tend to see things in black or white, good or bad, right or wrong. By their very nature, they call others to stop living in shades of gray and move up to a higher standard.

As the name of this Life Language implies, Movers are amazing action people who seem to be in constant motion, making things happen. The life of a Mover usually goes through some ups and downs on their way to success, but it will seldom be boring. They do not give up until they hit a gusher, although they may drill a few dry holes along the way.

The race is on—and Movers rush to the finish line.

THE MOVER INTELLIGENCE: INSTINCTIVE-KINETIC

Mover is the number one communication style of entrepreneurs. In many cases, Movers start more than one business during their lifetime. It's not unusual for them, once a business is up and running, to turn it over to someone else, then start another business. For them, the challenge to take on new things may never end. Mover characteristics could be found in a leader, supervisor, or employee, male or female.

THINKING "OUTSIDE THE BOX"

Most Movers tend to rely on their instincts. They have "street smarts" and enjoy exciting, risk-taking activities. They think outside the box and are full of creative ideas. A Mover senses or sees the next wave and knows how to make more things happen by accident than most people do on purpose.

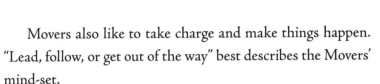

Movers also like to take charge and make things happen. "Lead, follow, or get out of the way" best describes the Movers' mind-set.

> It is important for young entrepreneurs to be adequately self-aware to know what they do not know.
> —Mark Zuckerberg
> co-founder and CEO of Facebook

MOVER SYMBOL FROM NATURE

What best represents the Mover would most likely be a wild horse or wild mustang. These horses are quick, intelligent, sure-footed, courageous, risk-takers, and resilient. To a degree, they are untamable and unpredictable. When treated well, they can become loyal cutting horses. You would never see them pulling wagons or plowing fields.

Some of these horses have become legends, with books and screenplays written about them—like Cloud of the Pryor Mountains in Montana, Misty of Chincoteague, Virginia, and the cavalry horse Comanche, the only known survivor of the Battle of the Little Bighorn. Some wild horses have gone on to become racing champions.

MOVER COLOR

The color that best describes a Mover is fire engine red. Red is the color most associated with energy, determination, power, heat, strength, and action. Red suggests boldness and excitement; it's not easily ignored or overlooked. Red is also a passionate color. The Mover language is one of great passion; that comes from the strength of their communication style.

Movers respond to life's events automatically and instinctively. They usually move rapidly into action when needed. While they are moving, their *feelings* become engaged and they are further energized even more. They often *rethink* the action or conversation once the "event" is over.

If their behavior does not meet their own standards and expectations, they can be quite hard on themselves. By nature, they tend to be hard on others, but ultimately, they are even harder on themselves.

POSITIVE CHARACTERISTICS OR ATTRIBUTES OF MOVERS

6%

Those with Mover as their first or primary language will have most or many of the following characteristics. Those with Mover as their second or third language, and so on, will have fewer of these characteristics. *For more detail, see Appendix A.*

Courageous	Risk taker	Innovator
Bold	Likes excitement	Forward thinking
High standards	Decisive	Entrepreneurial
Tenacious	Visionary	Change maker
High energy	Results-oriented	Direct
Hyper-vigilant	Proactive	Persuasive
Strong personality	Pioneering	Verbal
Honest	Introspective	Sensitive
Truthful	Assertive	Creative ideas
Perceiver	Dramatic	Introspective

Approximately 6 percent of the population speak Mover as their primary Life Language.

FOUR KEYS TO SUCCESSFUL COMMUNICATION

1. Answer Their Filter Question: *"What Is Your Motive?"*

A Mover has a filter that first sees a situation, conversation, or problem, then asks the question, "What is your motive?" or "What is your agenda?"

Movers like direct, to-the-point communication. It would not be a good idea to go to a Mover coworker and say, "What time are you leaving work today?" The Mover's filter response to this is, "Why are you asking me that question?"

A direct approach would bring a more successful outcome. For instance, the coworker could say to the Mover, "I have some client proposals that I desperately need to get out today and I'll probably have to work late. If you have some time, I could sure use your help."

Movers want to know the bottom line.

2. Meet Their Need From Others: *Action and Congruency*

For a Mover, all talk and no action is very frustrating. Movers really thrive where action is allowed and expected, and new ideas are appreciated. In relationships, they want congruency—it is very important that your words and actions line up together. In other words, "Do what you say and say what you do."

If you say you will get a project done on time, but then leave work early or show up late without a valid excuse, a Mover boss will be concerned. Even if you complete the project and meet the deadline, the Mover may think you didn't see it as a priority. They may even ask, "Why did you wait until the last minute to turn this in?"

Knowing the assignment was a *priority* project, the Mover boss will wonder why you didn't turn it in *before* the deadline. They might question your motives and even think that your words and actions just don't line up.

Movers need and expect you to follow up quickly—*beating deadlines!* When we see through the Mover's filters, we can see why completing a job on time seems like it's been delivered late.

3. Encourage Their Passion: *Innovation*

Movers are not happy in an environment that stays the same. They are gifted with the ability to change, rearrange, and refine things, systems, procedures, methods, territories, departments, or personnel. Movers are creative idea people who are seldom, if ever, satisfied with the status quo. They like to improve almost anything by innovating.

If you work with a Mover, it is important to not take their desire to make changes personally. And if you give the new idea, procedure, or method a chance, you will generally find that their ideas overall are quite good.

> Find that thing that you are super passionate about…
> and do it. —Mark Zuckerberg

4. Validate Their Character: *Courage, High Standards*

The Mover's key character strength is courage, particularly courage for high standards. They face life head-on, with courage and purpose. They have the courage to change the status quo. They have the character and perseverance to reach out and achieve the highest standards in their chosen profession.

Movers also have a respect for what's fair and right, especially when it involves the underdog.

> Courage is the most important of all the virtues because without courage, you can't practice any other virtue consistently.   —author Maya Angelou

ESSENTIAL TRAIT TO CULTIVATE: MAINTENANCE

Movers are fast-paced visionaries and innovators who enjoy making things happen. When one project is completed, they are ready to move on and start a new project.

Generally, one of the Mover's greatest weaknesses is a willingness to not maintain a project and deal with its day-to-day, routine activities. Thus, Movers must develop the trait of *project maintenance* or be in a position that allows this responsibility to be delegated but not ignored.

SUCCESS HABIT TO DEVELOP: BEING A FINISHER

Movers either need to develop a habit of handling daily details and finishing what they start, or work with someone who is a daily, detail-oriented person.

If they are not careful, Movers will start new projects while present projects are still left unfinished. A Mover in a supervisory or leadership position would want to staff others to handle the small, routine tasks that must be done.

CASE STUDY OF A MOVER

Dr. Bourke asked Life Languages International to profile his entire staff, including himself, at his medical clinic. His wife took the KLLP at their church and told him about the program.

Dr. Bourke was a highly successful emergency room doctor for over five years when his associates and advisors began telling him, "It's time for you to slow down and start your own private practice. You need to spend more time with your family and start working on your personal financial portfolio."

He decided to take their advice and go into private practice. After all, it all seemed to make sense.

When Dr. Bourke called us, his very successful private practice was just three years old. It was growing so fast that he had just added two more doctors and increased his nursing staff. It appeared that his life was perfect.

But as he spent time with his patients, Dr. Bourke found that many of them wanted to tell him *all of their problems*. As their doctor, he felt it was important to be a good listener. But the truth was, he didn't like sitting and listening to their problems. He tried to politely cut them off without offending them, but it still seemed like he was doing a lot of listening, making him late for each subsequent appointment.

Dr. Bourke thought the solution might be to see fewer patients personally and have the other doctors handle the rest. He decided he would do more administrative work for his practice.

But being an administrator proved to be even more frustrating for him. He didn't enjoy all of the paperwork and management details. Besides, his office manager was an excellent administrator and very good with detail work.

Dr. Bourke excelled at overseeing the staff, motivating them, and bringing in more patients, but it wasn't long before he realized that even this was not enough. He felt unfulfilled.

When our paths crossed, Dr. Bourke was seriously considering leaving medicine altogether. "Why continue doing something I no longer like?" he kept asking himself.

When Dr. Bourke took the KLLP, he discovered his first Life Language was Mover.

"Wow!" he exclaimed. "No wonder I found emergency room medicine so exciting and rewarding."

He loved the fast pace and not hearing patients complain about problems that were unrelated to their reasons for being in the ER. And no paperwork!

Dr. Bourke's greatest skill was his ability to make fast and intuitively accurate, lifesaving, medicinal decisions. As he continued to read about his communication style, he realized that for the first time in his entire medical career, he understood himself and the choices he had made.

Going into private practice was great for some of his friends, but not for Dr. Bourke. Now, he's back doing what he loves—saving lives as an amazing emergency room physician.

Courage is not simply one of the virtues, but it is the form of every virtue at the testing point, which means at the point of highest reality.

—author/theologian C.S. Lewis

DISTRESS FLARES: ADA

1. **Attack**

2. **Demand**

3. **Attack again**

A distress flare experience or incident from a Mover may be occur during one conversation or take place over two or more days, depending on the circumstances. Remember, these are *dysfunctional* indicators that something isn't quite right for the Mover. They will say things like:

Attack: "Hey, have you done what I asked you to do?"

Demand: "I need it now, so stop everything and get this done!"

Attack: "Where is it? You don't have it finished yet!?"

Sometimes, if a Mover feels they have been especially hard on the other person, they will set up a fourth flare:

Apologize: "Thanks so much. I'm sorry I was so hard on you. I should have known you would finish it in time."

> We may express our distress flares in our second or even our third Life Language, so it is important to be aware of all of the different ones and be able to identify which flares we tend to operate in when under stress.
> —Anna Kendall

LEADERSHIP STYLES

+ Courageous, with high standards for honesty and integrity

+ Innovative, with creative ideas

+ Usually very good at explaining the vision and the big picture

+ Strong motivators

- Willing to identify and confront problems, bring change, and accept risks

- Both proactive and reactive

- Desirous of good communication but may not slow down for it unless requested

- Have expectations of action and results from others

Movers who are leaders need others on their team so they can empower those who are detail-minded and willing to take actions necessary to see results.

OTHER LEADERSHIP TRAITS

A cultural philosophy of success: "We will be successful as long as we keep rapidly moving forward, are willing to take risks, and outwork and outthink the competition."

An entrepreneurial organizational structure: Movers like to start new things. As a leader, a Mover may have many old and new things going on at the same time. Wise Movers will have staffs that can keep things going while they make new things happen.

When in health, the Mover leader will be a focused innovator who makes things happen successfully.

When in distress, the Mover leader will be fragmented and forceful, with many things left unfinished.

POSSIBLE PROFESSIONS

Mover is the number one language of entrepreneurs. They are not usually software or computer designers, but they often own a software company. They can also be a CEO, supervisor, or department head. They may have careers in the military, law, marketing, sales, law enforcement, or construction. They can work as an emergency medical technician, lifeguard, emergency room doctor or nurse, business owner, coach, pastor, or public speaker. Movers like work that involves action, changing the status quo, and stimulating excitement, with just an element of risk.

> Talk to people in their own language. If you do it well, they'll say, "God, he said exactly what I was thinking." And when they begin to respect you, they'll follow you to the death.   —former Chrysler CEO Lee Iacocca

CLUES FOR COMMUNICATING

The following clues are helpful when communicating with a Mover:

+ *Verbal clues*: Listen for action and accomplishment words: "Let's make this happen" or "Here's what we need to do." Movers may interrupt you if they think you're rambling or bringing up too many unnecessary details. They tend to make statements for shock value, saying things like, "I've got five minutes; what's the bottom line?" or "Cut to the chase."

+ *Non-verbal clues*: Movers may make very quick movements or do multiple things while you are talking to them. They may appear to have very short attention spans unless they are really interested. You may think you're not getting a Mover's full attention, but they seldom miss a single point. They may move in and out of your conversation to talk to others. They're easily bored

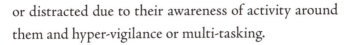

or distracted due to their awareness of activity around them and hyper-vigilance or multi-tasking.

+ *Visual clues*: A Mover's decor is often functional and low maintenance, although they may have games and gadgets scattered about. Movers often have definite ideas about style, form, and function. Their office walls may feature prints depicting action or adventure. Their style of dress is usually sharp, but uncomplicated.

+ *Affirmation phrases*: Always be prepared when communicating with a Mover. Know what you want to say and say it. *Give bullet point facts* before details, then carefully observe how much detail the Mover wants. Their facial expressions will usually tell you. Offer positive solutions. Tell them, "I appreciate your time and won't take much of it." State your reason or motive for conversation, such as, "I'd like your insight on this situation…"

+ *Behavior that can frustrate a Mover*: It may help to remember these behaviors with the acronym BEERS: blaming statements, excuses, explaining, rehashing, or serving up the past. Inconsistency and incongruent behavior or speech are very frustrating to a Mover.

+ *Ways to motivate a Mover*: Get right to point with any business encounter or discussion. Don't spend too much time off-topic. Always try to provide bottom-line benefits or consequences. If you have an innovative plan or approach, present it. Let the Mover know you appreciate their cutting-edge decisions or achievements and you want to participate in their plan or innovation.

People who are Movers just *have* to be on the move. They are called forward by what they see as possibilities in the future. Their forward-thinking, innovative gifts pull them out of the past and even the present to vistas "out there somewhere," new and often untested or never before tried.   —Anna Kendall

EXAMPLE OF A FAMOUS MOVER

Having been a sickly boy, with no natural bodily prowess, and having lived much at home, I was at first quite unable to hold my own when thrown into contact with other boys of rougher antecedents....I felt a great admiration for men who were fearless and who could hold their own in the world, and I had a great desire to be like them.

—from *An Autobiography by Theodore Roosevelt*[3]

We are confident that President "Teddy" Roosevelt had Mover as his primary language. Rather than letting childhood asthma limit his life, he embraced boxing, wrestling, walking, climbing, horseback riding, and other activities. He reformed the corrupt U.S. Civil Service Commission as well as the New York City Police Department. Tackling any challenge with enthusiasm and vigor, Roosevelt was an accomplished writer, a fearless Rough Rider, and a dedicated naturalist. As president, he established many new national parks and forests, began construction of the Panama Canal, and expanded the Navy fleet. He won the 1906 Nobel Peace Prize for his negotiations that brought an end to the Russo-Japanese War.

3. http://www.gutenberg.org/files/3335/3335-h/3335-h.htm.

Campaigning for the New York governorship in October 1898 before a large, boisterous crowd, Roosevelt declared:

> A soft, easy life is not worth living, if it impairs the fiber of brain and heart and muscle. We must dare to be great; and we must realize that greatness is the fruit of toil and sacrifice and high courage....For us is the life of action, of strenuous performance of duty; let us live in the harness, striving mightily; let us rather run the risk of wearing out than rusting out.[4]

---

4. http://www.theodore-roosevelt.com/images/research/txtspeeches/604.pdf.

NOTES

5

DOER:
GETTING IT DONE RIGHT

THE DOER ICON

The initial Doer icon features a to-do list that's been stamped "completed," an eye for the Doer's attention to detail, a hand checking off an item on a list, and another hand holding a hammer. The new icon retains the hammer because Doers are usually very good with their hands and will hammer away at things until they have completed the assigned task, regardless of its size, nature, or the time involved to complete it. And, no matter what, they say, "It has to be done right!"

The Doer name is written letter-by-letter on steps leading upward, symbolizing the way in which Doers generally work their way up the ladder in business, one step at a time.

The to-do list is essential to a Doer's day-to-day existence. There's nothing that a Doer likes better than seeing the hand-stamped "completed" symbol on their task list. They derive immense pride and internal satisfaction as they check off each item. Doers like to manage their lives, so their lists keep them on track and well-organized.

Most Doers like short-range projects that can completed or accomplished in a day, week, or weekend. If a project is too long and requires an enormous amount of time, they may have trouble staying "on task." They like to see items on their list checked-off with regularity.

Doers are observant, able to see the practical details and physical needs around them, details that others may overlook or just not notice. Not only do Doers *notice* these details, they are generally delighted to *jump in* and help others meet these practical needs.

THE DOER INTELLIGENCE: PRACTICAL-KINETIC

Doer is the *number one* communication style of the self-employed. Often, Doers are small business owners with no employees or very few. They enjoy working with their hands. Many are engineers, accountants, dentists, or carpenters. They are practical, hands-on people who see the needs around them that others often miss or totally overlook.

To finish or not to finish is never the question for a Doer. They *love* to finish their tasks or assignments!

Have you ever been around someone who seemed to truly *enjoy* being busy? If you're a "people-watcher," you'll quickly notice that a Doer is the individual who *arrives early* for a meeting or event and is one of the *last to leave!* It's not because they enjoy visiting with everyone; they are busy helping with whatever is needed, including getting snacks ready, making coffee or pouring drinks, or printing copies of handouts and passing them out. The Doer takes copious notes during a meeting. When it's over, as everyone else is leaving, the Doer is usually found picking up the empty coffee cups and generally helping to put the meeting room "back in order." Doers generally don't make a big deal of this activity. It's almost like it's part of their DNA— they're doing what comes naturally.

> Action may not always bring happiness…but there is no happiness without action.
> —Benjamin Disraeli, former British prime minister

DOER SYMBOL FROM NATURE

Like Doers, beavers are busy, diligent, hard-working, and seemingly tireless. Typically, a Doer is unstoppable when attacking a project. Beavers, too, have been observed working continually until they are finished. They chew down trees, drag them to the water, construct dams, and create dens for their families. They provide food and take care of the practical needs for not only for themselves and their family, but for the entire beaver colony.

Beavers' dams create wetlands that attract fish, ducks and other birds, frogs, turtles, and other creatures. In fact, many species coexist with the beavers inside their dams, especially during cold months. Although they can be a nuisance for farmers and other landowners, these busy creatures play an important role in nature.

Doers are often "as busy as a beaver."

> Anna and I were recently eating lunch at a restaurant when a man came over. "Aren't you folks the Life Languages people?" he asked. "You came to our company a year or so ago and profiled all of us. I can't remember the name of my Life Language, but I do remember that I was a beaver! You all *just profiled* everyone at the company where my wife works and you told her she was a dolphin. Now, after twenty-seven years of marriage, I can finally communicate with her and understand her!"

DOER COLOR

Orange is the color associated with a roaring fire, the flame of a candle, and, of course, the sun, with its invigorating effect on our world. Orange represents growth, expansion, perseverance, and diligence; it stimulates and energizes us. That alertness and energy are easily observed in Doers. Orange creates an *environment of productivity* and the Doer Life Language is filled with productive abilities.

Each morning, the beauty of the rising sun and its rich, orange color give the typical Doer a brand-new day for accomplishments.

> It is wonderful how much may be done if you are always doing.   —President Thomas Jefferson

POSITIVE CHARACTERISTICS OR ATTRIBUTES OF DOERS

Those with Doer as their first or primary language will have most or many of the following characteristics. Those with Doer as their second or third language, and so on, will have fewer of these characteristics. *For more detail, see Appendix B.*

10%

Attentive	Detail-oriented	Enjoy serving others
Dependable	Loyal	Have difficulty saying "no"
Diligent	Finisher	Sees immediate needs
Obedient	Enjoys receptive tasks	Likes routine
Organized	High energy	"Now" oriented
Punctual	Good maintainer	Hands-on
Trustworthy	Helpful	Stay busy
Make fast decisions	Work well behind the scenes	Makes lists
Like short-range goals	Observant	Seldom depressed

About 10 percent of the population speak Doer as their primary Life Language.

FOUR KEYS TO SUCCESSFUL COMMUNICATION

1. Answer Their Filter Question: *"Are You Doing Your Share?"*

Doers see the practical things that need to be done. It can be taking out the trash at home, filing papers, returning phone calls, making coffee, or keeping things in order.

Sometimes, if a Doer is the only one on the team or in the family who speaks "high Doer," others may not even notice that these things need to be done. If they do notice, they can easily ignore that responsibility without it bothering them. Doers see these responsibilities as practical needs, as if a spotlight was shining directly on them. Internally, they will wonder why others don't realize these things.

If you are dealing with a high Doer, get into a habit of looking for practical things to do that would please them. If possible, also look for practical words to describe various tasks and duties.

2. Meet Their Need From Others: *Appreciation and Action*

In both their personal and professional lives, Doers want to receive appreciation for a task well done. Since they themselves like to stay busy, they don't appreciate others who don't seem to be accomplishing anything. They can incorrectly perceive someone who is thinking or planning as doing nothing! This is where communication is extremely important.

Finished tasks and accomplishments need to be acknowledged; whether you're the boss or a coworker, you need to let the Doer know that you are pleased. It's important to compliment the finished task, not the person. Remember, all of us have needs that, when met, cause us to feel appreciated, motivated, and understood.

3. Encourage Their Passion: *to Finish!*

Doers are task-oriented and like to work from a list. They are fulfilled when they can finish short-term goals and check that task off their list. Doers become very frustrated if they are given numerous tasks and not enough time to finish them.

Doers thrive when their passion to finish is fulfilled. When given a list, they will naturally do their best to complete the tasks in a timely way. To get maximum results from a Doer, when given task has long-term goals, subdivide it into short-term, accomplishment goals.

4. Validate Their Character: *Trustworthiness*

It is wonderful when someone can be trusted to do what they say they will do. There is great and satisfying comfort in being with that person. Doers are trustworthy, but they need to know that others are doing their share, their work is appreciated, and they have enough time to complete the tasks they are given.

Discuss openly and honestly any previously unspoken "practical expectations" that the Doer believes need to be addressed and put them all on the table for discussion. Doing this will prevent future misunderstandings. Whether you are a Doer, or you are working with a Doer, this action step is essential and will keep your business or home running smoothly.

> Continuous effort, not strength or intelligence, is the key to unlocking our potential.
> —Winston Churchill, former British prime minister

ESSENTIAL TRAIT TO CULTIVATE: DELEGATION

Because Doers are usually so good at doing so many things, it is often difficult for them to delegate assignments. They must commit to making it a serious personal goal, especially if they want to move into positions of leadership.

Doers don't typically want to delegate work because they often think, "By the time I tell him what to do and show him how to do it, I could have already done it myself—and know it was done right." Unfortunately, this mind-set is common to

Doers. However, those who move up into management positions can learn the art of delegation and we know many successful Doers who have accomplished this.

SUCCESS HABIT TO DEVELOP:
THINK LONG-TERM/LOOK AHEAD

Doers can get so caught up with what they think is an *immediate* need that they sometimes miss the long-term, important needs.

For example, a Doer supervisor at a large company was frustrated that the break room looked so bad. The walls were dirty, so he decided to come in over the weekend and paint them. "A fresh coat of paint would make the room look better and would make the employees feel better," he reasoned. And it did just that.

But this Doer supervisor failed to first check with the property manager. He just saw a need and *filled it*. He took care of an immediate problem. Unfortunately, he failed to check on the more important, long-range changes that were in the works. The company was planning to take out a wall to make the break room bigger.

DOER CASE STUDY

Sandra, an engineer working for a large company in Texas, was very frustrated with her job. She thought she wasn't connecting with the other engineers because she was the only female in the department. After we profiled them, however, we discovered some very interesting information.

The engineers had two basic functions: They were responsible for providing technical information for the sales department and often went out on sales calls; and they were responsible for the technical designs and completing the products in a timely manner. Everyone in the engineering department had the same responsibilities.

Sandra complained to us that most of the engineers talked more than they worked and they didn't seem to be very concerned about finishing jobs on time. The clients would get angry, then the chief operating officer (COO) would complain to the engineers, and the problems just seemed to be getting bigger and bigger. *No one was happy.*

The COO, a Mover, asked us if he should just *fire the whole department and start over.* He knew they were all highly qualified, but just didn't know why they were having so many production problems.

After looking at the department's KLLPs, the problem became very clear to us and the COO. Sandra was the only one who had Doer as her first Life Language. Two of the other engineers had Influencer as their first Life Language—they were relational with good people and sales skills. Another engineer had Mover as his first Life Language; he was creative and liked to make things happen, but was not detailed-minded. Two more engineers had Contemplator as their first Life Language; they were brilliant, but not very time conscious or people-oriented.

After a couple days of discussion with us, the COO made a major decision. He divided the engineers into two departments, with some overlapping duties and responsibilities, but also distinct ones. One department would focus on sales support and design. The other would focus on design, product completion, and quality control.

Sandra was promoted as supervisor over both departments. Not only was she a Doer who was very detailed-minded, she was also a hands-on perfectionist who was well-organized and absolutely dedicated to finishing assignments on time. Her second Life Language was Shaper, enabling her to see, plan, and schedule long-range projects to meet critical deadlines.

The COO was prepared for complaints from the other engineers, but after they all understood their KLLPs, they agreed Sandra was the perfect leader and they supported her. It's been five years and we are still working with that company. They are all still a highly successful and functioning team.

> When Doers respond to life events, they first start with action. They "see a need and meet it." To them, whatever needs to be done is *obvious* and usually practical. They are programmed mentally to respond. Their response to a situation is more automatic than reached by a reasoning process. They get more assignments and projects completed than most people because of their ability to take immediate action.   —Anna Kendall

DISTRESS FLARES: MAG

1. Martyred

Doers may feel like they are the only ones who are doing anything practical and productive, especially if they are the only Doer in the department, team, or family. They can't understand why others are overlooking the needs they see quite clearly. Doers often fail to consider that others are focusing on what is important to them from their own personal perspectives. When under stress, it's easy for a Doer to feel martyred.

2. Accusatory

If the stress continues, it's not unusual for the Doer to express frustration. They may say things like, "No one else ever does anything around here. Why can't some of you ever clean up the break room?"

3. Grumbling

Doers then fall into complaining to others about all that they do and how little others do. Grumbling is a form of criticism that is not directed to any specific person. Doers just walk around complaining.

Remember, distress flares go up when the person has moved into unhealthy behavior—usually due to not dealing with stress in a healthy way. Doers need to receive appreciation and action in order to avoid these flares.

A few who do are the envy of many who only watch.
—Jim Rohn, entrepreneur and motivational speaker

LEADERSHIP STYLES

+ Hands-on

+ Focused on the practical and immediate needs of a job

+ Committed to creating an organization that is functional and dependable

+ Setting the pace of the team

+ Organized

- ✦ Exhibiting trustworthy traits that become evident to employees, clients, coworkers, and competitors

- ✦ Teachers; their form of training is most likely to have others work alongside them as they teach by doing

- ✦ Happy with "to-do" lists, both for themselves and others

OTHER LEADERSHIP TRAITS

Cultural philosophy: "Each of us has a job for which we are responsible. We must be diligent and tenacious about completing our *daily* tasks. The long-range tasks will then take care of themselves."

An organizational structure for tasks and processes: Doers prefer that all employees have job descriptions and training for predictable tasks. They like the team, tasks, and procedures to have structure. Most importantly, they expect everyone to finish their tasks.

When in health, Doers are excellent, practical finishers. They are great at making sure all of the details are completed.

When in distress, Doers can be non-functioning martyrs. In any job or environment where they are not allowed to finish a task before other projects are started, the Doer may so stressed that they are stuck or frozen. They can sometimes *just stop and shut down* altogether.

POSSIBLE PROFESSIONS

Doers can be chief financial officers, certified public accountants, small business owners with no or few employees, engineers, draftsmen, nurses, carpenters, tailors, doctors, dentists, accountants, software developers, computer technicians, teachers, lawyers, jewelers, bookkeepers, craftsmen, secretaries, office managers, or work in manufacturing or construction. Doers enjoy work that has definite, controllable parameters. They are usually good with hands-on, repetitive work.

> The secret of getting ahead is getting started. The secret of getting started is breaking your overwhelming tasks into small, manageable tasks...then starting on the first.   —author Mark Twain

CLUES FOR COMMUNICATING WITH A DOER

+ *Verbal clues*: Doers are not prone to a lot of small talk. They are generally quite professional. They'll politely ask, "What can I do for you?" They are comfortable discussing tasks that need to be accomplished. Listen for action words. Their motto could easily be, "If it needs to be done, just do it!"

+ *Non-verbal clues*: Doers may take notes while listening to you. They are purposeful multi-taskers and tend toward crisp, direct movements. They may check their watch often to make sure they are on schedule.

+ *Visual clues*: They usually have offices with a functional décor and everything kept in meticulous order. Even if they use computers and smart phones, they also have wall or desk calendars (sometimes both!), lists, and dry erase boards.

+ *Affirmation phrases*: "Your work was excellent. Thanks for completing it on time!" "I really appreciate your organizational skills." "Here is our long-range goal for this year. Would you help me break it down into weekly and monthly short-term goals?" "You are amazing at keeping all the details under control."

+ *Behavior that can frustrate a Doer*: Taking longer to do assignments than you agreed to. Wasting time on non-business chatter. Missing a deadline or not doing something you promised to do.

+ *Ways to motivate a Doer*: Talk in systematic, step-by-step language. ("First we need *this*, then we can begin *that*.") Be willing to help them not lose sight of the "big picture." Doers tend get too involved in the day-to-day details. Provide guidelines for action.

EXAMPLE OF A FAMOUS DOER

I have one life and one chance to make it count for something…. My faith demands that I do whatever I can, wherever I am, whenever I can, for as long as I can with whatever I have to try to make a difference.

—Jimmy Carter[5]

Born in 1924, Jimmy Carter leads a busy and active life. He began working in his father's store at age ten. He studied engineering, graduated from the U.S. Naval Academy, and worked on the Navy's nuclear submarine program. When Carter's father died, he returned to Plains, Georgia, to restore the family's peanut farm. Active in politics, he was elected governor of Georgia in 1970, then president in 1976. America was buoyant, having just celebrated its 200th anniversary, but the

5. http://www.nobelpeacelaureates.org/pdf/Jimmy_Carter.pdf.

aftermath of the oil embargo, the Iranian revolution, and the hostage crisis all left their mark.

Carter soldiered on. His negotiations with Israel and Egypt led to a historic peace treaty. After he lost his reelection bid, Carter continued to champion peace, human rights, and the eradication of deadly diseases. He started volunteering for Habitat for Humanity in 1984 and has helped to renovate more than 4,300 homes. In 2002, he was awarded the Nobel Peace Prize.

Carter has written more than thirty books and still teaches Sunday school. At home, Carter cooks, does the dishes, swims, builds furniture, paints, and walks daily.[6] He also fishes and hunts. We're pretty sure Carter is a Doer because he keeps busy doing practical things and finishing what he starts.

> Failure is a reality; we all fail at times, and it's painful when we do. But it's better to fail while striving for something wonderful, challenging, adventurous, and uncertain than to say, "I don't want to try because I may not succeed completely."   —Jimmy Carter[7]

---

6. Kevin Sullivan and Mary Jordan, "The un-celebrity president Jimmy Carter shuns riches, lives modestly in his Georgia hometown," *Washington Post*, August 17, 2018.
7. Jimmy Carter, *Sources of Strength: Meditations on Scripture for a Living Faith* (New York, NY: Three Rivers Press, 1997).

NOTES

6

INFLUENCER: LOVING LIFE—AND PEOPLE

THE INFLUENCER ICON

The original Influencer icon features two clasped hands, evoking relationships; a heart for the emotive intelligence category; confetti and fireworks, symbolic of the way Influencers celebrate life and people; and a quill and artist's pallet to represent creativity.

The new icon features clasped hands in front of a heart because Influencers are great people persons. They tend to have many friends and acquaintances, due to their diplomatic, tactful, and friendly personalities. They also like to bring agreement between individuals and groups. Influencers are persuasive and can get contracts signed.

There's joy, fun, and enjoyment wherever Influencers go and they're seldom bored or boring.

Influencers are usually good at either creating or appreciating music, poetry, art, sculpture, books, architecture, decorating, dance, and other artistic endeavors.

They also have the ability to see logical solutions to life's situations, which often surprises others. They *feel* first, and then *think* rapidly and logically.

> Influencers encourage us to be the very best we can be. They accept us as we are and then encourage us to become more. They bring spontaneity and joy to our hearts.   —Anna Kendall

THE INFLUENCER INTELLIGENCE: RELATIONAL-EMOTIVE

Do you know people who easily and naturally encourage those around them? They seem to have the art of forming relationships and people enjoy being with them. An Influencer boss or supervisor can point out your mistakes and offer advice on correcting them in a positive way.

Influencers are often natural-born motivators and we find them in many areas of leadership, from sales and marketing to corporate CEO and president of the United States.

Influencers are usually quite verbal. In fact, we often quote Garrison Keller, who makes a strong Influencer statement when he says, "I talk and talk till I think of something to say." However, they not only talk easily and diplomatically, they think fast on their feet, so what they say is usually either important, clever, informative, inspirational, or entertaining. Influencers like to enjoy life!

INFLUENCER SYMBOL FROM NATURE

Like Influencers, dolphins are fun-loving, smart, social, playful, and relational, generally living in a community. They excel in finding ways to enjoy themselves, such as jumping out of the water, racing beside boats, playing games, and splashing each another as they frolic about.

And yet dolphins are hard-working, serious about catching fish (which they generously share with others), and good at caring for and training their young. They have been known to leap in and defend or rescue whales, other animals, and people.

Dolphins are so smart that the U.S. Navy has trained them to rescue lost swimmers or locate underwater mines.

INFLUENCER COLOR

Bright, sunshine yellow cannot easily be missed or ignored—and neither can an Influencer. Their dress and personality just exude cheerfulness. Yellow is associated with luminosity and radiant light. It symbolizes spirituality, enthusiasm, optimism, quick intellect, intuitiveness, and playfulness, all fitting descriptions of Influencers.

Yellow is often used to stimulate learning. The Influencer's usually sunny disposition helps to make them popular and successful.

> Influencers respond to life first with feelings, then immediately by thinking. They automatically and almost simultaneously access their feelings and their thinking. Those who don't understand this about Influencers miss the depth of this communication style.
>
> —Anna Kendall

POSITIVE CHARACTERISTICS OR ATTRIBUTES OF INFLUENCERS

14%

Those with Influencer as their first or primary language will have most or many of the following characteristics. Those with this as their second or third language, and so on, will have fewer of these characteristics. *For more detail, see Appendix C.*

Relational	Encouraging	Charming
Creative	Future-oriented	Think win-win
Enthusiastic	Logical	Flexible
Positive	Verbal	Joyful
Outgoing	Optimistic	Fun
Seldom depressed	Persuasive	Comfortable
Networker	Accepting	Diplomatic
Make fast decisions	Offer solutions	Has many friends
Innovative	Intuitive	Inclusive

About 14 percent of the population speak Influencer as their primary Life Language.

FOUR KEYS TO SUCCESSFUL COMMUNICATION

1. Answer the Filter Question: *"Are We Communicating?"*

Influencers want to connect and establish a relationship, no matter how short or long one may be. Their communication hits the mark and their excellent people skills ensure that they build a rapport.

2. Meet Their Need From Others: *Affirmation*

Influencers can be seen and heard giving to others what they themselves need: affirmation. They will be the first to acknowledge, "Job well done," "That was a great speech," "Your report was outstanding," and so on. They need to hear affirmation in return. If there is no one around who can do this for the Influencer, they may provide this affirmation for themselves through self-talk.

3. Encourage Their Passion: *to Encourage*

Influencers have an innate and natural passion to encourage others and motive them to do better or their best and become all that they can be. Influencers look for the best in others and want them to grow into their potential.

4. Validate Their Character: *Enthusiasm*

When the first three points are met, the Influencer character quality of enthusiasm is strengthened. Otherwise, the Influencer has to really work at being enthusiastic. Even so, when an Influencer is feeling down, it doesn't last long and they will soon become enthusiastic again. They find depression boring. Keep in mind, their key trait is that they love people and life.

> Please don't get the mistaken idea that an Influencer is fluff or shallow because they are enthusiastic about life. Since they feel then think so rapidly, they have incredible depth, come up with amazing steps of action, are well informed on many subjects, and usually have the right word at the right time for any and all occasions.
>
> —Anna Kendall

ESSENTIAL TRAIT TO CULTIVATE:
DEVELOP INTEGRITY OF WORDS AND PROMISES

Because Influencers are so positive in their approach to life, goals, and priorities, they often think they and others can do more than they really can. Plus, they don't like to disappoint people. So an Influencer might tell a customer, "Yes, we can deliver this by the time you need it," go back to the office, and then find out that the engineering department can't possibly meet that timeline.

If you are an Influencer and have not overcome this tendency, set up very simple safeguards for yourself. Before you make any promises, check with others to make sure it's doable. If you want to schedule a lunch with a client, make sure you have the date open on your schedule. The Influencer's positive attitude means they want to make things happen, but they need reality checks.

SUCCESS HABIT TO DEVELOP:
BALANCE TALKING AND LISTENING SKILLS

Influencers are generally quite verbal and usually have something to contribute on most subjects. They also seem to supernaturally know the correct steps of action to solve any problem.

But all talk and no listening is a true relationship destroyer—just the opposite of what Influencers desire. They can learn to balance both of these skills, but it will take effort.

> So often, people are unhappy and they don't understand why. They just leave the job, and they and management never know the real reasons. Being the right person in the right position is critical.
>
> —Anna Kendall

INFLUENCER CASE STUDY

Working in the wrong position can be deadly!

During an afternoon break at a workshop for an insurance company, one of the employees asked us to look at her Kendall Life Languages Profile because she had some questions. Her primary Life Language was Influencer, so we said she probably had many friends, was optimistic, liked to encourage others, liked to talk, and so on. Then we asked her what her position was. We were shocked to learn she was a payroll clerk.

"Does that mean you work in a cubical, have little interaction with other employees, and have to do rather tedious, repetitive work?" we asked.

"That pretty well describes it."

We told her she might be happier working with the public. She quickly responded, "Oh, please don't mention that to anyone! This is the best job I've ever had and I'm a single mom. I really need this job."

We agreed not to say anything and continued with the workshop.

A few months later, the head of HR called and asked if we remembered an employee named Julie in payroll. We had—it was the Influencer.

"Well, you won't believe this, but a week ago, she had a major heart attack and she is only forty-eight. The doctors were shocked."

The company was holding Julie's job for her, but the HR head was looking over Julie's KLLP and wanted to discuss it. As we started to explain it, she said, "From this, it looks like she should be in a position dealing with the public, doesn't it?" We emphatically agreed.

Six months later, after recovering from her heart attack, Julie was placed in a lateral position working with the public, where she thrived.

We're not saying that being in the wrong position caused her heart attack, but the stress of doing something she was trained and qualified to do, *but not gifted or happy doing it* certainly contributed. According to the *American Journal of Hypertension*, depression, stress, and anxiety can increase a person's risk of cardiovascular disease.[8] We need to enjoy our work and our relationships.

> Do something you are passionate about, do something you love. If you are doing something you are passionate about, you are just naturally going to succeed. Life is too short to work where you lack the passion to be there.
>
> —Mary Barra, CEO of General Motors

DISTRESS FLARES: DAE

Since Influencers need affirmation, their distress flares are:

1. Deny

They will deny that there is anything wrong, or that they did anything wrong, or that it is or was a big deal, or… You get the picture.

---

8. https://academic.oup.com/ajh/article/28/11/1295/2743312 (accessed Sept. 21, 2018)

2. Argue

Influencers are usually quite good at debating. If they are in distress, they will argue. They may also be accusatory.

3. Escape

If things stay stressful and others are argumentative, an Influencer will look for a way to escape, at least for a short time. They may leave the office or go for a coffee break, just getting away from the situation.

If this behavioral cycle continues and is not dealt with in a healthy manner, the Influencer will predictably keep going back and forth through the cycle. They can stop the flares through self-awareness, making a choice to tackle the problem, or by receiving help from others.

LEADERSHIP STYLES

+ High profile leaders who believe in sharing the spotlight

+ Committed to growth of self and those they lead

+ Motivational, inspirational, and persuasive

+ Encouraging

+ Proactive

+ Future-oriented

+ Focused on solutions

+ Relational

OTHER LEADERSHIP TRAITS

Influencers tend to articulate a vision for others to follow. They also have these traits:

Cultural philosophy: "If we build relationships, through good communication, looking for positive solutions that allow us to work together toward mutual goals, we will be able to outperform anyone."

An Influencer organizational structure: Network. "We build networks and support one another throughout the community."

When in health, Influencers are motivators.

When in distress, they are manipulators.

POSSIBLE PROFESSIONS

Influencers can be CEOs, supervisors, department heads, politicians, evangelists, public speakers, artists, musicians, authors, decorators, architects, diplomats, lawyers, or business owners. They can work in marketing, sales, advertising, radio, or television. Influencers will enjoy any profession that is people-oriented and creative.

CLUES FOR COMMUNICATING

+ *Verbal clues*: An Influencer is a "people person," socially interactive and very personable with coworkers and clients. They make each person feel special, give compliments and encouragement, and use inclusive words. An Influencer will sincerely ask, "How are you?" or "What's new with you?" They will tell you that you look great. If you have an issue, they say, "I know just the person you need to meet" because they love to connect people.

Influencers are encouraging and optimistic; they enjoy people and life.

+ *Non-verbal clues*: Influencers may be running late. They have fun pictures, photos, and items on their desk. They easily give you a hug or a pat on the back. They may extend both hands to clasp your hand in greeting. You may feel like you have known an Influencer for a long time, even when you haven't. They generally put people at ease. They will come out from behind a desk to sit with you.

+ *Visual clues*: An Influencer's desk may seem unorganized or disorderly. They are prone to creative environments and colorful décor. They generally dress with a flair. Influencers like sound and color, visual and audio stimulation.

+ *Affirmation phrases*: Reaffirm their abilities and be encouraging. "Visiting your office is the bright spot of my day" or "You really are a pleasure to be around." Tell them, "I know you have creative thinking and ideas." Express interest in and affirm their personal tastes, fashion choices, and decisions.

+ *Behavior that can frustrate an Influencer*: Keep in mind, Influencers believe you can deal with negative situations in positive ways. So they are frustrated by negativity or complaining, especially when others are not looking for solutions. They also don't appreciate people who give in to self-pity rather than seeking understanding or actual help.

• *Ways to motivate an Influencer to action*: Ask them to be a resource and contribute their ideas. If you have energy and passion about a project, product, or procedure, they will be more apt to buy into it with their own energy and passion. Let the Influencer use their creativity. They love networking, connecting people, enthusiastic presentations, and building excitement.

EXAMPLE OF A FAMOUS INFLUENCER

The future is ours to build. Surmounting the risks and the fears of some may be difficult, but I'm convinced the challenge is worth it. The greatest victories come when people dare to be great, when they summon their spirits to brave the unknown and go forward together to reach a greater good.　　　　　—Ronald Reagan[9]

President Ronald Reagan had the charismatic, fun-loving, persuasive, optimistic, and encouraging characteristics of an Influencer. He is often remembered for two things: ending the Cold War and being "the Great Communicator."

Born in Illinois in 1911, Reagan attended Eureka College on an athletic scholarship, majoring in economics and sociology. He was active in sports, served as student council president, and acted in college plays. After graduating, Reagan went to work as a sports announcer in Iowa, then moved to California, took a screen test, and began his movie career. After appearing in more than fifty films, he hosted a television show, then jumped into politics.

9. Ronald Reagan Presidential Library & Museum, "Remarks to Chinese Community Leaders in Beijing, China," April 27, 1984 (https://www.reaganlibrary.gov/sspeeches/42784a).

Reagan had a plain way of speaking that hit home with people. And his cheerful nature burst forth, even when confronting an opponent. While running for reelection and debating Walter Mondale in 1984, Reagan said, "I will not make age an issue of this campaign. I am not going to exploit, for political purposes, my opponent's youth and inexperience." Mondale laughed, along with the audience. Reagan was then seventy-three.

> I wasn't a great communicator, but I communicated great things, and they didn't spring full bloom from my brow, they came from the heart of a great nation— from our experience, our wisdom, and our belief in principles that have guided us for two centuries.
>
> —Ronald Reagan[10]

10. Ibid., "Farewell Address to the Nation," Jan. 11, 1989.

NOTES

7

RESPONDER:
FEELING ENERGIZED

THE RESPONDER ICON

The new icon retains the chief elements of the original one: an extended hand holds a heart, representing the emotive intelligence category and the Responder's desire to reach out to others with care and compassion. Other elements of the initial icon are a quill and pen, harkening to the Responder's creativity; a diamond design, signifying a multifaceted personality; and goal posts, since Responders tend to be goal-oriented.

Responders have a natural desire to touch the lives of those in need and help them ease their emotional pain, especially during a crisis.

The two emotive Life Languages, Influencers and Responders, lead to expressions of artistic creativity—or an appreciation of it—such as music, poetry, art, sculpture, books, architecture, decorating, and dance. They have touched the hearts and minds of individuals around the world, all the way back to the beginning of recorded history.

Responders have the potential to accomplish great good because they have the ability to care so deeply. But sometimes, Responders can be like a diamond in the rough, needing others to believe in them and help them discover their own potential. Responders are known for wearing their emotions on their sleeves. When they are aware of someone in need, they immediately feel compassion and will respond with great care and concern. Unfortunately, some individuals will play on the Responders' sympathy and take advantage of them. Responders must guard their hearts against this.

When Responders are passionately committed to something, they tend to wrap themselves around it—whether it's a project, task, person, or job.

THE RESPONDER INTELLIGENCE:
RELATIONAL-FEELING

Do you know people who are sensitive and aware of others around them? These people seem to instinctively know when someone is sad, hurt, or angry. Responders know when *something is wrong* even when the individual in crisis has not said anything and their facial expressions haven't displayed pain or distress. Responders are very protective of people they work with and care about.

Responders may be sensitive, but they are by no means weak. Responder is the number one Life Language for men and women who play contact sports, especially football quarterbacks, tennis players, and boxers. The word *emotion* means "energy in motion." *Feelings* energize Responders and those who play sports do so with seemingly endless energy. It is a language of steel and velvet—strong and sensitive.

> If I could reach down in my heart, I would say I'm sorry for every unkind word and thought I ever had.
>   —Terry Bradshaw
>   TV sports analyst and former quarterback

Responders tend to put passion into everything they do. To be successful, they need to feel passionate about their job, their product, or their mission. Doing something they *believe in* is their life's blood.

Responders respond to life first with feelings, then with their actions, and then by thinking. They generally prefer to get consensus *before* making a major decision.

RESPONDER SYMBOL FROM NATURE

Like Responders, collies are loving, affectionate, caring, brave, energetic, protective, regal, and often heroic. Responders live to rescue people who are hurting or seemingly lost. Similarly, a collie can fearlessly rush to save those they love, even when it puts them in harm's way. Collies seem to have the incredible ability to show unconditional love and acceptance. They are sensitive and nurturing yet strong and protective.

RESPONDER COLOR

The Responders' color, violet or purple, has been the color of royalty for thousands of years. Purple dye was rare in ancient times, so it was prohibitively expensive and commoners were often forbidden to wear purple garments.

Purple is also associated with honor, spirituality, self-esteem, creativity, imagination, affection, and passion. The Purple Heart is awarded to members of the armed forces who are wounded in war or given posthumously to the next of kin. This combat medal signifies great personal sacrifice.

POSITIVE CHARACTERISTICS OR ATTRIBUTES OF RESPONDERS

33%

Those with Responder as their first or primary language will have most or many of the following characteristics. Those with Responder as their second or third language, and so on, will have fewer of these characteristics. *For more detail, see Appendix D.*

Accepting	Verbal	Second Language visible
Relational	Available	Easily shakes hands or hugs
Reaches out	Compassionate	Protective
Physically responsive	Many friends, but few close	Likes to please
Peacekeeper	Creative	Humility
Athletic	Sensitive	Prefers friends one-on-one
Gentle	Enjoys contact sports	Supports underdog
"Now" oriented	Likes approval	Loyal
Sincere	Emotional energy	Carries burdens

About 33 percent of the population speak Responder as their primary Life Language.

Responder is the Life Language that's most frequently spoken as a first communication style. If you speak Responder and Doer, you will speak the preferred Life Languages of *over half* the population.

> The world is full of hurting people and Responders desire to help others by making their emotional pain go away. Whether this is your first or last Life Language, we should be thankful for these caring people who want to help us grow and overcome obstacles in our paths. —Anna Kendall

FOUR KEYS TO SUCCESSFUL COMMUNICATION

1. Answer Their Filter Question: *"Do you really care… about me and those I care about?"*

By letting Responders know that you do care, they will, in a sense, lay down their lives for you. The old expression, "I don't care how much you know, till I know how much you care" must have been said by a Responder.

2. Meet Their Need From Others: *Unconditional Acceptance*

This is not the same as unconditional approval. We can accept another person without approving of their actions. For a Responder, this message needs to come through loud and clear. Responders are sensitive and any angry, critical, or disapproving words or remarks can be devastating. Although you can correct them, the words you use should be carefully thought out beforehand.

Responders also need to be understood and listened to. In important relationships, a strong degree of trust is vital. The Responder needs to know that they can share feelings and know they will be understood—and not judged. They feel connected when you both share your feelings. In the workplace, it is important that supervisors and executives learn to manage Responders by understanding this. Responders care so deeply about others that they can be very valuable and trusted employees, coworkers, and friends.

3. Encourage Their Passion: *to Please and Protect*

Responders have an innate and natural passion to be pleasing to others and protect others. In one company we worked with, a departmental supervisor was known for defending and protecting his employees. He expected to be treated fairly by his own bosses and wanted those under him to be treated fairly, too.

If a boss sends signals that nothing a Responder employee ever does is quite good enough, they will eventually leave. Conversely, if the boss sends the message that he is pleased with both the work and the Responder, the employee will be unstoppable.

4. Validate Their Character: *Compassion*

Healthy Responders are sensitive to the needs, hurts, or problems around them and their natural compassion is often all that's needed to bring healing and keep an organization running smoothly.

Since Responders care deeply and show compassion, they are greatly needed throughout the world. We believe that is why there are more Responders than any of the other 7 Life Languages. Responders have tremendous potential for good.   —Anna Kendall

ESSENTIAL TRAIT TO CULTIVATE: RESPONSIBILITY

We do not mean to imply that Responders are irresponsible. However, those who speak this as their primary Life Language often juggle competing priorities. Coupled with the Responders' desire to please is a tendency to operate in the "now." If they have not disciplined themselves, they can easily get behind in their work and may not understand why. For example, a Responder gets ready to leave for an appointment that was scheduled a month ago when a client comes into the office. The Responder becomes concerned about helping the client and ends up missing the scheduled appointment or showing up late.

For many Responders, having to reschedule appointments is a regular occurrence. To remedy the problem, they can force themselves to adhere to a strictly defined time schedule. This forced regimentation to a schedule and calendar of events is often a trait a Responder has to cultivate and work at continuously if they are going function effectively, both at home and at work.

SUCCESS HABIT TO DEVELOP: PROFESSIONALIZE, DON'T PERSONALIZE

Responders are personally very sensitive. If they receive criticism or are left out of an event or meeting, they can feel that something is wrong with them. Some small, internal self-talk can help them "professionalize" rather than "personalize."

They must come to the realization that *everyone* is criticized occasionally or left out of meetings. And we all make phone calls and send texts or emails that are never returned.

The main point for the Responder is to learn objectivity— the ability to see the big picture and both sides of a situation. The world does not revolve around us, nor does everything that happens in it involve us. It's okay! We can let it go and move on.

RESPONDER CASE STUDY

The board member of a large nonprofit organization in California asked us to profile all of their executive staff and board members. He had some concerns about the new CEO and wanted to know how to help him. Going over everyone's KLLPs, we discovered the CEO was a very high Responder. In fact, his second Life Language was forty points away. It was like he stayed in Responder and if he went to his other communication styles, he seemed to *fall off a cliff* and couldn't access them easily.

This organization worked with the homeless and had multiple locations. The CEO was wonderful working with the men and women who came there for help. He was sensitive to their needs, their hurts and brokenness, could encourage them to believe in themselves, and offered them great hope. He was also an amazing fund-raiser.

But he was not trained to run the business aspects of this organization. He had been a good friend of the former CEO and had risen through the ranks due to his success in helping people directly. He also had a tendency to believe people who came to him with their solutions to problems without looking at the big picture or taking the time to evaluate all of the information.

So we worked with this Responder CEO and the board to use his strengths in caring for the homeless while his staff handled the paperwork and managed the resources, billing, and budgets. He gave them oversight and insights into the people they served. Both he and his team were loyal to each other and the organization established a great working environment. We revisited them and retrained them in the Life Languages every three months, then every six months. We continued to be in contact with them on an annual basis, or when there was a conflict or critical hiring need.

After several years, the Responder left the CEO position and the board replaced him with a very capable Shaper/Mover. His leadership style was different, but he was adept at long-range planning and promoting the organization's growth and success. We think the ongoing Life Languages training over the years helped to ensure a smooth transition.

DISTRESS FLARES: CAD

1. Complain

Responders who are going into stress tend to unleash a series of angry, personal complaints about current tasks. For example, they might say, "Why didn't you do what I asked?" or "You knew this was important to me, but you didn't do it" or "It doesn't seem to matter what I ask of you." Some of these complaints may be unspoken and internalized, but deeply felt when a Responder is in stress. Unfortunately, Responders tend to internalize their personal or job issues, so they may create turmoil in their workplace. Once in distress flare mode, a Responder can start to have feelings that may not even be related to the problem at hand or relevant to the situation.

2. Accuse (Which Often Seems Like Attack)

After a while, if and when the initial complaints don't work, a Responder may start attacking a coworker, friend, or family member with sentences that begin with, "You never" or "You always..." The attacking accusations can get stronger and more verbally painful, especially for the person who's being attacked. The Responder may muse upon and relive these feelings.

3. Depression Begins

The Responder, after accusing or attacking, can then start to feel helpless and hopeless, then depressed. If the attack cycle becomes a frequent pattern, the Responder will feel stuck. They may need to get professional help to deal with this continuing problem. A Responder feels things very deeply, both good and bad. Extreme highs and extreme lows are not unusual. Although Responders have amazing potential for good because they care and feel so deeply, they may nevertheless unintentionally create unhealthy problems for themselves and those around them if they hold on to negative feelings. They can unknowingly sabotage their own personal relationships and careers.

LEADERSHIP STYLES

+ Deeply loyal

+ Compassionate

+ Concerned about the well-being of individuals under their charge

+ Passionate about a cause or goal and wrap themselves around it, relentless in their pursuits

+ Sensitive to the needs of others

+ Protective

+ Peace-keepers

OTHER LEADERSHIP TRAITS

Cultural philosophy: "We have a job to accomplish, so let's support and take care of each other as we achieve our goal."

Organizational structure: Teams. And Responders, more than any other Life Language, may adopt the leadership style of their second language.

When in health, Responders are altruistic.

When in distress, they are self-absorbed.

POSSIBLE PROFESSIONS

Responders can be CEOs, artists, musicians, authors, decorators, architects, advertising salespeople, school teachers, counselors, social workers, receptionists, supervisors, psychologists, therapists, pastors, nurses, family doctors, and professional athletes, especially hockey players, football players, and boxers.

ANOTHER RESPONDER CASE STUDY

Responders are "second language visible," meaning their communication style is generally so clear and transparent that their second Life Language shines through. In light of this, as well as the fact that Responder is the primary Life Language of a third of the population, we wanted to share another case study about a Responder.

We profiled the seven senior partners at a small law firm. James's profile initially surprised everyone in the room. His first communication style was Responder, with 5 points to his second language, Shaper. He was the only one measuring more than 50 percent intensity in the Responder language. The other partners saw James as a high Shaper but not as a Responder. They discussed this unexpected phenomenon.

"Well, we do tend to give James all the clients who seem to have emotional problems because he handles them better than the rest of us," one lawyer said.

"I guess what we all see is how strong his Shaper is," another noted. "But now that I think about it, all his clients just love him and the rest of us don't get that same response from *our* clients."

Everyone agreed that James was a focused, strategic, and organized lawyer who wins his cases. But they also realized that whenever anyone at the firm had a personal problem, they went to James.

As they studied the filter, passions, and needs of a Responder, they said, "We don't treat James that way." We asked James if he would like to be communicated to as a Responder and he said yes. The other partners were stunned by this revelation.

Later, talking to James privately, we learned that he felt devalued and somewhat unappreciated. Even though he was a successful lawyer earning big fees, he had talked to his wife about leaving the firm. Now, since the other partners had agreed to treat him as a Responder, James recommitted to them. He remains happily at that firm today.

CLUES FOR COMMUNICATING

+ *Verbal clues*: A Responder is a sensitive, compassionate person who is concerned about you and all who are on his team or in his family. Listen for more feeling words rather than thinking words: "How do you feel about this decision?" or "Let me share with you." Responders like to keep the peace and look for peaceful ways to handle intense situations. They are relational and prefer one-on-one contact with others.

+ *Non-verbal clues*: They naturally reach out and touch an arm or hand or give the person they are talking to a pat on the back. They must be careful of such physical touches in today's corporate environment. Responders can easily laugh with others and cry when feeling pain with them. Responder men are strong enough to show they can be tender and caring.

+ *Visual clues*: Warm office decor with photos and mementos of family and friends. They may display interests in art, music, writing, or sports, and have motivational sayings on the walls of their office.

+ *Affirmation phrases*: Responders take a personal and compassionate interest in others. They will ask, "How are you? And how is your family?" Coworkers really appreciate it when a supervisor remembers the names of family members. Be careful how you phrase a question to a Responder. For example, don't ask, "What do you think about…?" Instead say, "How do you feel about…?"

+ *Behavior that can frustrate a Responder*: Asking them to make a decision *right now*. Unless one of their other Life Languages, such as Mover or Influencer, scores high for them, they would rather take their time and get a consensus. The more confident they are, the faster they will make a decision. Also, making too many demands at once on a Responder will result in no resolutions. They don't do well in an atmosphere of conflict and confusion.

+ *Ways to motivate a Responder*: Show care and concern before you demand action. Once a Responder knows you care, they will all but lay down their life for you. The motto of Responders could easily be "I don't care how much you know until I know how much you care." Again, when dealing with Responders, use words such as *feel, share*, and *care*. Responders feel connected when you listen to them and share some things about your own feelings. Or even better, share some things about what or who they care about.

EXAMPLE OF A FAMOUS RESPONDER

Spread love everywhere you go. Let no one ever come to you without leaving happier.   —Mother Teresa[11]

Born in Albania in 1910, Mother Teresa (Saint Teresa of Calcutta) took her formal religious vows at age twenty-one, choosing to be named after the patron saint of missionaries.

---

11. https://www.catholic.org/clife/teresa.

After working as a teacher in India for nearly two decades, in 1948, she received permission to leave her convent to live full-time among "the poorest of the poor" in Calcutta. Two years later, she founded the Missionaries of Charity to look after people who could not care for themselves and had no one else.

Mother Teresa and her nuns fed them, clothed them, washed them, prayed for them, and gave them a place to live... or die with dignity, in comfort, rather than in the city streets. Today, the Missionaries of Charity includes more than five thousand religious sisters and seven hundred homes serving the poor and marginalized around the world.

Although some called Mother Teresa "a living saint," she showed her humanity as well. She got angry if she felt she was intentionally left out of a meeting. If her nuns were denied work visas, she took it personally, saying, "I will take my girls away."[12] She was also called "a benevolent dictator" because she had a way of making people do things her way. If she received an invitation to see the pope, she would bring others with her—and no guards could deter her.[13]

Responders care deeply about the hurts and pain of others, as Mother Teresa did. She also had a Responder's passion when protecting her nuns or the poor people they served.

> It is not how much we do, but how much love we put in the doing. It is not how much we give, but how much love we put in the giving. —Mother Teresa[14]

12. Hector Welgampola, "Mother Teresa's Anger Had a Subtle Message: Veteran Journalist Recalls His Two Encounters with Mother Teresa," *Matters India*, August 2016.
13. Leo Maasburg, *Mother Teresa of Calcutta: A Personal Portrait: 50 Inspiring Stories Never Before Told* (San Francisco: Ignatius Press, 2011).
14. Mother Teresa, *No Greater Love* (Novato, CA: New World Library, 1997).

NOTES

8

SHAPER:
LEADING THE PACK

THE SHAPER ICON

A hand moves a chess piece on a board with squares labeled "A" and "Z" for the original Shaper icon. There's also a globe, indicative of the Shaper's approach to life, with big dreams and large visions, and a chart with Rodin's *The Thinker* superimposed on it.

The new icon features a globe that's been opened to reveal chess pieces and bar graphs in the mind of a head that represents the cognitive intelligence category. All are indicative of the Shaper's strategic thinking and planning capabilities.

Shapers may not especially like to play chess, but their mind-set is very much like that of a chess player—always strategically thinking about the next move. They tend to see the whole picture from beginning to end as they mentally map out their strategy for completing an assignment.

During the planning process, some Shapers will actually think about the end of a project in order to start it. In their mind, working backwards—from the end rather than the beginning—makes more sense. Regardless of which way they think about an assignment, they want to see the whole picture in their mind before beginning.

Shapers often have plans for the next year, a five-year plan, a ten-year plan, and even longer term. They are career-oriented and progressively move up to greater levels of success in both their professional and personal relationships.

THE SHAPER INTELLIGENCE: VISIONARY-COGNITIVE

The Shaper is often the "leader of the pack." Natural leaders, visionaries, and organizers, they envision and carry out local or worldwide programs of peace, progress, and relief. They are the planners and leaders who help us accomplish great short-term or long-term goals, pursue magnificent dreams, and keep our eyes focused on our ultimate destinations.

Shapers are usually the ones who rise to a position of leadership, often without even trying. Whether it's becoming a CEO, department head, PTA president, or neighborhood watch organizer, they may be surprised when they realize they've been placed in charge.

Plans are nothing; planning is everything.

—President Dwight D. Eisenhower

SHAPER SYMBOL FROM NATURE

The "king of the jungle," lions are strong, independent leaders, capable, patient, regal, protective, and organized. Like lions, Shapers are typically respected by coworkers and those they meet. Lions  like to have their entire pride divided into "departments"—those who growl, those who hunt, those who chase, and those who enjoy the feast. They are strategically skilled and successful providers through group action that's well-organized. Lions, like Shapers, have a grace and an excellence of life that evokes admiration from followers and even from the competition.

SHAPER COLOR

Deep, royal blue or indigo is a color that's often associated with visionary leadership, success, high aspirations, knowledge, and even power. Shapers have the ability to reach high and far, growing, expanding, and taking all of us who know them along on their journey to success. Indigo is a color of great depth and Shapers add depth to their lives through their planning, organization, leadership, and achievements.

Often, Shapers have a quiet aura about them that generates a state of satisfaction within themselves and projects a feeling of quiet dignity. This is not an internally arrogant state of mind nor an attitude of constantly needing to pat themselves on the back. Rather, Shapers are comfortable in their thought processes and believe in the importance of pursuing excellence.

POSITIVE CHARACTERISTICS OR ATTRIBUTES OF SHAPERS

Those with Shaper as their first or primary language will have most or many of the following characteristics. Those with Shaper as their second or third language, and so on, will have fewer of these characteristics. *For more detail, see Appendix E.*

Organized and efficient	Enjoys planning	Pursues excellence
Sets long-range goals	Endurance	Visionary
Responsible	Natural born leader	Tolerant
Delegator	Future-oriented	Develops others
Successful	Communicates ideas, plans	Looks for results
Single-minded and focused	Learns from past	Decisive
Uses charts, graphs, lists	Discreet	Values appearance
Expects preparedness	Time-sensitive	Dislikes most small talk
Watches bottom line	Embraces change	Could be workaholic

Approximately 19 percent of the population speak Shaper as their primary Life Language.

> If you think you can, you can. And if you think you can't, you're right. —Mary Kay Ash
> founder of Mary Kay Cosmetics

FOUR KEYS TO SUCCESSFUL COMMUNICATION

1. Answer Their Filter Question: *"Do You Have a Plan?"*

Shapers think everyone should have a plan for their life, career, and family. If they think you *don't* have a plan, they may want you to join their plan. If a Shaper finds out you don't have your own personal plans or goals, they may just dismiss you as not having your life together. A few Shapers may be willing to help you devise a plan if they believe you are amenable to the idea.

2. Meet Their Need From Others: *Support and Agreement*

Shapers don't want you to be a "yes person" because they are almost always open to differences of opinion. However, Shapers are leaders and their critics sometimes take potshots at them. When you're on the front lines or are a ground-breaker, you often become fodder for those who have never taken a risk or "stepped outside the box" in their life.

Shapers need to feel the assurance that those who care about them and work with them also support them and are in agreement with the vision and direction of the assignment or mission.

3. Encourage Their Passion: *to Lead*

Shapers lead others automatically and naturally with planning, delegating, and *developing* others. They seem to instinctively know which person is best suited for which position, whether it's at work, in the community, or at home. They tend to consistently be able to get the right people to do the needed jobs.

In situations where there's clearly no one in charge, Shapers will rapidly size up the situation, gather facts, access the pros and cons, and then, if appropriate, assume responsibility and start planning and delegating.

4. Validate Their Character: *Patience for the Plan*

Shapers are not necessarily patient with people and often need to work on developing that trait. But while Shapers may be impatient with others, they almost always have great patience for the plan or plans. This is why they can have goals for five or ten years—or more.

They easily and automatically set long-range goals and then break them down to "doable tasks" for themselves or others, as needed. They pull together what is needed and organize or chart out the growth patterns. Whatever the time length, a Shaper will deliberately keep everything moving forward to successfully complete the plan.

> One only gets to the top rung of the ladder by steadily climbing up one at a time, and suddenly all sorts of powers, all sorts of abilities which you thought never belonged to you, suddenly become within your own possibility and you think, *Well, I'll have a go, too.*
> —Margaret Thatcher, former British prime minister

ESSENTIAL TRAIT TO CULTIVATE: SENSITIVITY TO OTHERS' EMOTIONAL NEEDS

Shapers can be so focused on the *plan* that they may overlook the emotional or relational needs of others in the process. It's not that Shapers are cold, indifferent, or uncaring, but their naturally intense personal makeup to stay focused on goals and plans can cause others to perceive them as such.

To ensure success, people need to know that Shapers are not taking them for granted. Shapers are usually self-disciplined, so it is helpful for them to remember to stop occasionally and express understanding or caring when communicating with other people.

SUCCESS HABIT TO DEVELOP:
RELAX, REFLECT, AND RELATE

The development of this habit is much like developing the essential trait of stopping or pausing long enough to let others know that you truly care. The truth is, we all need other people.

Shapers need to relieve stress by finding ways to *relax* away from work, such as exercising, doing crafts, going for a walk, or gardening. Shapers also need to slow down and *reflect* on the overall health of those they are leading, as well as their own health, as Shapers can become workaholics.

And they generally must slow down to remember to *relate* to others in ways that don't involve their plans. They should express interest in their coworkers, their families, and their needs. It's easy for Shapers to focus on the plan and overlook the very individuals who are helping them complete it.

SHAPER CASE STUDY

We all have dreams, plans, and opportunities when communication is the key ingredient to *maximize the moment*. Being fluent in the 7 Life Languages will prepare you to be in the right place at the right time with the right message, thus ensuring your success.

Robert, a young, ambitious man with a large oil company and a Life Languages student, called to tell us of this experience:

> One of the senior partners, whom I interact with the most, seems to demonstrate many of the characteristics of the Shaper communication style. He had not taken the KLLP, so I wasn't sure what his first communication style was, but I recognized that his Shaper was

high. When we have staff meetings for my department, this senior partner is organized, efficient, focused, and very dedicated to long-range plans and goals.

One afternoon, as I was walking down the hall to my office, I passed this senior partner, who paused and asked, "How are your projects going?" I wasn't sure if he really wanted to know or was just being friendly, passing time, but I felt this might be my moment, so I quickly said, "Sir, things are going great with my clients since I've been charting and graphing time lines and long range goals. I'm finding I'm more on top of things, focused, and much more efficient. I'm meeting all my deadlines. Thank you for the great ideas you shared with us."

I was unsure if I came across as too eager, but in the next weekly meeting, the senior partner addressed me by name. Since then, he has often called on me during staff meetings.

Robert took advantage of a chance encounter to maximize the moment and make his mark by speaking the Shaper Life Language to his boss.

CHIPMUNKS VS. ANTELOPES

Talking about strategy, former U.S. House Speaker Newt Gingrich said lions instinctively know that focusing on big game, such as an antelope, is better than catching a small animal such as a chipmunk for a quick little snack. Small creatures like rabbits and chipmunks are fast and difficult to catch. If a lion *did* go after one of these little animals, he would probably be tired from the chase and still hungry. On the other hand, by bringing down an antelope, he has enough food for himself and the other lions.

Shapers often think like a lion. They don't waste time on chipmunks or little tasks. Instead, they tend to identify the real goals in both life and business, setting their sights on the next big challenge. We have found this analogy to be a very effective way to organize our own focus on business each day. We have used it as a way to engage front-line managers and associates to better understand the peril of not knowing what their "antelopes" really are and how to fend off the natural tendency to chase what's immediately in front of them: the chipmunks.

Shapers seem to understand that true success occurs when you postpone immediate gratification and focus on long-range goals. It's something we all should work to embrace.

DISTRESS FLARES: CET

1. Criticize

Shapers are very capable of overseeing tasks and work assignments. They desire excellence from themselves and others, so if things are not going as expected, the Shaper can become very critical. If they just stop and communicate, most internal problems can be corrected. Unfortunately, while Shapers tend to be patient when creating and overseeing a plan, they can often become very frustrated with people around them. Learning to set aside time regularly to show caring, grace, and understanding to a deserving staff is absolutely necessary if a Shaper's relationships are going to remain intact and close.

2. Eliminate

At one large organization, the Internet went down several times and there were a couple minor departmental issues. Without warning, the CEO walked into the information technology department and fired everyone on the spot. He then began to outsource all of his IT needs. Communication with people in that department would have been a valuable alternative before making what appeared to be a very impulsive decision. The CEO's erratic behavior caused a great deal of unnecessary anxiety for employees in other departments.

3. Take Over

Often, a Shaper in distress will take over a job or even the entire department as he corrects or eliminates those individuals who, in his opinion, "shouldn't be there!" This kind of drastic action can shake up an entire organization unnecessarily. In all fairness, the Shaper *may* make the organization better and stronger, once the changes are completed, but in the meantime, the other employees are left in quiet despair...perhaps even feeling broken.

Fortunately, most Shapers are seekers and learners. Once they learn the power of communication through the Life Languages, they handle distress in healthier ways.

LEADERSHIP STYLES

+ Natural leaders; placed in any environment, they often rise to a position of leadership without trying

+ Visionary

- Will stay focused on the vision, no matter how long it takes

- Seek excellence

- Organized

- When healthy, they will share praise and recognition

- Very orientated on return on investment (ROI)

- Will move forward and take those who share the vision with them

- Are good at developing others to become all that they can be

- Focused on the future

Shapers are leaders who *visualize final results* (goals) and are able to direct people, plans, and resources to their successful completion. They enjoy an expansive managerial role. Shapers delegate well; they check back for results and hold each person accountable for their part of any project or assignment.

OTHER LEADERSHIP TRAITS

Cultural philosophy: "Each of us has a role to play to which we are held accountable. Let's do our jobs, stick with the plans, and we will accomplish our goals."

A Shaper organizational structure: the buck stops here!

When in health, the Shaper leader will be an excellent developer of people, plans, and organizations.

When in distress, the Shaper leader will display calloused ambition.

POSSIBLE PROFESSIONS

As natural leaders, Shapers can be CEOs, CFOs, specialists, department heads, administrators, analysts, lawyers, pilots, architects, engineers, medical doctors and specialists, and business owners. They can enter politics or serve in the military or government. They often have graduate degrees.

CLUES FOR COMMUNICATING

The following clues are helpful when communicating with a Shaper:

+ *Verbal clues*: Shapers use thinking, planning, or accomplishment words. They will say, "Our goals include..." and "Looking toward the future..." They will ask, "Do you have a plan?" or "How will this help us reach our goals?" or "What are the bottom-line results?"

+ *Non-verbal clues*: Shapers are not interested in small talk and they will attempt to direct the conversation to something substantive. They have a focused, professional attitude.

+ *Visual clues*: Shapers are very organized and may prominently display awards or certificates in their offices. Books reveal their personal interests. Shapers often prefer formal, tasteful furniture in cherry wood, mahogany, or leather. There's minimal clutter on their desk. They may have photos of famous people on their walls. Shapers often have massive offices, a large working staff, and charts and graphs of progress and goals.

+ *Affirmation phrases*: Shapers want to hear about plans, goals, and delegation of tasks. Affirm their ability to

lead: "Since you are considered a leader in the community..." or "It is so great to see how you are leading this
company..."

+ *Behavior that can frustrate a Shaper*: The perception that
an individual lacks direction or vision and doesn't have
a plan. Shapers don't understand people who seem to
wander through life without knowing where they are
going.

+ *Ways to motivate a Shaper*: Ask what their goals or plans
are. Explain how you desire to support their plans. If you
can, show or explain how you can fit into the Shaper's
plans and tell them how you can support and encourage
them. Affirm that their plans are worthwhile.

Shapers need support and agreement. Whether you are
the boss, a coworker, or a friend, Shapers feel affirmed when
you acknowledge the front line they are on making far-reaching
decisions. You will gain a Shaper's confidence when you display
your support.

Like Movers, Shapers are out front making decisions that
bring change. They often get criticized by people who don't
understand their goals or don't like change. They need people who support their vision and are in agreement, not as a
"yes" person but as someone who recognizes the value of their
leadership.

EXAMPLE OF A FAMOUS SHAPER

To be an effective leader, you have to have a manipula-
tive streak—you have to figure out the people working

for you and give each tasks that will take advantage of his strengths. —General H. Norman Schwarzkopf[15]

"WAR!" In January 1991, Americans were glued to the news of Operation Desert Storm as our troops and our allies pursued Saddam Hussein and his army six months after Iraq invaded Kuwait.

During his first press conference, General H. Norman Schwarzkopf described, in great detail, the step-by-step opening moves of the war, using graphs, charts, maps, and diagrams. Organized and confident, General Schwarzkopf quickly oversaw and directed the build-up of 700,000 coalition troops, including more than 540,000 U.S. forces.

Although we don't know what his KLLP would have been, we believe Schwarzkopf's first Life Language was Shaper and his second was Mover. *Time* Magazine described him as a man "with a John Wayne swagger" and the growl of an 800-pound grizzly bear.

Schwarzkopf commanded, directed, supervised, and oversaw every phase of the war. He assembled an excellent command group, pulling together the right people, the right equipment, and the right countries, which he gave the authority to direct their own areas of responsibility.

This visionary military leader could see the war's outcome from the very first day of battle and he effectively set up an hour-by-hour, day-by-day strategy to reach his desired goal. Kuwait was liberated in six weeks and "Stormin' Norman" returned home to a hero's welcome.

---

15. H. Norman Schwarzkopf, *It Doesn't Take a Hero: The Autobiography of General Norman Schwarzkopf* (New York, NY: Bantam Books, 1992)

You learn far more from negative leadership than from positive leadership. Because you learn how not to do it. And, therefore, you learn how to do it.

—General H. Norman Schwarzkopf

NOTES

9

PRODUCER:
CREATING ABUNDANCE

THE PRODUCER ICON

The initial Producer icon features a dollar sign, a gift-wrapped box, a welcome mat, and shafts of wheat, all in green and gold to indicate sufficiency and abundance. *The Thinker* is included to represent the cognitive intelligence category.

The new icon continues the theme for this category and in the Producer's mind, there's a dollar symbol, a target to indicate the way in which Producers hone in on the very best, and a wrapped gift.

Regardless of their income level, Producers have the ability to make and manage finances and resources very well. They usually retire with financial dignity and security.

Producers also have a very generous nature. They give philanthropically and are known for their hospitality. It doesn't matter if a Producer is (or isn't) expecting you in their home or office, you'll always feel welcome, as if they knew you were coming and were prepared for your visit.

They tend to have every aspect of their life on target. They like to be wrapped around their relationships and careers and seem to present both to the world as gifts.

Producers are usually the most *complete and balanced* of all the Life Languages.

THE PRODUCER INTELLIGENCE: RELATIONAL-COGNITIVE

Producers often live normal, seemingly quiet, and ordinary lives, even if they are financially comfortable or even wealthy.

Our Producer friend Patti knew how to make and manage money. She owned about twenty rental homes and was a very aggressive and successful real estate broker. For a short time, Patti tried to apply her micromanagement skills to the lives of her (successful) adult children. She quickly learned that was not a good decision!

One morning, we were having breakfast with Patti and the menu gave one price for a stack of pancakes and a *lower* price for the same size pancake stack plus two eggs. Patti asked the server about it, but she didn't know why the prices were like that.

Patti ordered the pancakes and two hard-boiled eggs and asked that the eggs be kept in their shells. After breakfast arrived, she got a to-go box and took the two eggs with her for lunch.

Whether dealing with large amounts of money or seemingly insignificant amounts, all Producers watch the bottom line and make choices accordingly.

PRODUCER SYMBOL FROM NATURE

Eagles build their nests to last a lifetime, high in the air on carefully selected cliffs, in a large tree, or even atop a cell phone tower. They return to the same nest year after year and improve or repair it for their new eaglets. The stability and durability of their nest construction underscores the quality of their workmanship.

Eagles mate for life and provide well for their young. They seem to enjoy sharing their parental responsibilities. Together, they train their young to fly. Eagles' keen eyesight and powerful bodies enable them to provide an abundance of food for their families.

Just as eagles use atmospheric storms to fly higher and faster, Producers typically use the storms in life to increase their resources and rise to new heights.

PRODUCER COLOR

Green is the middle meeting ground between the warm colors—yellow, orange, and red—and the cool colors—blue, indigo, and violet. Likewise, the cognitive Producer Life Language is midway between the kinetic and the emotive intelligences.

When appropriate, Producers can easily be oriented to both actions and feelings while remaining logical or cognitive in their thinking.

Green gives us the impression of something steady and soothing. The Producer radiates stability, endurance, growth, abundance, success, prosperity, and vitality.

POSITIVE CHARACTERISTICS OR ATTRIBUTES OF PRODUCERS

4%

Those with Producer as their first or primary language will have most or many of the following characteristics. Those with Producer as their second or third language, and so on, will have fewer of these characteristics. *For more detail, see Appendix F.*

Well-rounded individuals	Responsible	Strive for excellence
Make decisions easily	Personal growth-oriented	Stable
Sufficient	Good with action	Hospitable
Abundance	Gracious	Often good communicators
Give thoughtful gifts	Welcoming	Cognitively generous
Emotively graceful	Balanced	Prepared with resources
Courteous	Good money managers	Micro-manager
Thrifty	Looks for quality	Looks for savings
Resourceful	Good people skills	Exhibits vitality

Approximately 4 percent of the population speak Producer as their primary Life Language.

FOUR KEYS TO SUCCESSFUL COMMUNICATION

1. Answer Their Filter Question: *"Are You Generous and Are You Managing Your Life?"*

Producers tend to be generous, so they don't like to sense stinginess in others. Although they don't necessarily give to every needy person they meet or see—the way Responders are inclined to do—most Producers give to *worthy causes or people* when they know their gift will be handled wisely. Producers like to give *quality* gifts. They also enjoy treating their friends to dinner, a concert, or another special event. But if a Producer notices that all the gift-giving is one-sided, they will probably stop being so generous. In their minds, if you don't give them a gift in return, at least occasionally, you are failing to manage your life. Being cheap has nothing to do with it.

If Producers see a friend's life is out of balance, or out of control, they may simply *write off that person*. When first meeting Producers, if you start to immediately tell them all of your problems—without first letting them know you've worked out at least some of them—your *first* conversation with them will be your *last*. However, they will still be gracious toward you.

2. Meet Their Need From Others: *Appreciation for Their Gifts and How Well They Manage Their Lives and Resources*

Producers feel motivated and secure if they receive *appreciation* for all the amazing things (in their eyes) they do for others and the organization. They express their own appreciation often by giving gifts to coworkers, family, and friends. They are not generous solely to feel appreciated or receive attention, accolades, or praise. Rather, Producers would simply like an acknowledgement and a genuine thank-you from the recipient.

Producers give quality and thoughtful gifts; they feel loved or appreciated when they receive considerate gifts in return. The size or the cost of the gift isn't an issue. To the Producer, it's better to receive nothing in return for their generosity than to receive a hastily conceived, last-minute something with no thought behind it.

3. Encourage Their Passion: *to Manage*

Even as children, Producers like to manage as part of their realm of responsibilities. As adults, Producers like to manage projects, timelines, events, and especially resources and finances. They seem to innately know where money should go, how it can be used most effectively, and where the best deals are.

4. Validate Their Character: *Resourcefulness*

This key character trait shines forth in Producers like no other. Resourcefulness appears in most of their thoughts, actions, communication, and planning. They also look for this trait in everyone else!

ESSENTIAL TRAIT TO CULTIVATE: EMPOWERING OTHERS

Producers really like to find people they can trust and empower. However, they often have trouble turning assignments over to others because they can sense when someone lacks responsibility or has problems with follow-through.

Sometimes, Producers don't empower others because they like to keep control. A Producer who wants to be successful must seriously commit to working on ways to overcome their tendency to limit another who is more than capable of handling a particular assignment.

SUCCESS HABIT TO DEVELOP:
GIVE WITHOUT EXPECTATION OF GAIN

Healthy Producers like to give *appreciation* gifts to indirectly encourage and motivate employees to produce *even better* results for the company *and* let them know they are genuinely appreciated. *Unhealthy* Producers may use giving as a way to control another, such as persuading an employee to do a particular task. Unfortunately, when this happens, there are often strings attached.

We know a high Producer CEO who gave strings-attached gifts. For example, he gave his married adult daughter a new car with the stipulation that she and her family were to come to his home every Sunday.

PRODUCER CASE STUDY

In his late fifties, John was a vice president with a major oil company. He had always made a good income and managed it so well that there was no mortgage on either his home or his lakeside vacation house.

John's company was reorganizing, expanding, and considering the purchase of some new refineries. The human relations and personnel departments were placed under John, with the departmental supervisors reporting to him. Soon, John began to feel unfulfilled. He was hearing far too many employment and personnel problems. As a result, he was thinking about taking an early retirement. Although he was in a position to do so, he really didn't want to retire.

We had profiled all of the departments, including John's, so he called us to talk about his frustrations. It wasn't just the company's people problems that frustrated him; he also felt left out of the company's growth. His gifts and skills as a Producer were not being used. Prior to taking a job in the home office, John had traveled and dealt with refinery problems.

John met with the senior vice president to discuss his work history, his interests, and his KLLP. The company didn't want to lose John. They had placed human relations and personnel under him because he had good people skills and they knew he could do the job. However, it became clear that John's position was not challenging him. After several meetings, he was reassigned to the committee looking at buying refineries. John's financial skills and understanding of resources were so valuable that the company ultimately decided to build a new refinery rather than buy an older one with possible problems. John stayed with the company for twelve more years, feeling fulfilled and appreciated.

> Producers don't want to track where the money has gone. They want to give directions on where to send it. —Anna Kendall

DISTRESS FLARES: ROW

1. Restrict

When Producers see that excellence is not being pursued by a coworker or even someone at home, they may restrict that person's access to a particular assignment. It's not unusual for a very frustrated Producer to take the assignment away from the individual altogether. The Producers' mind-set is simple and direct in cases where they know coworkers are not trying to produce their best work. The Producer wants to see a project or assignment done right.

2. Organize

Sometimes, a Producer may completely reorganize a department. Some frustrated Producers may halt a project and take on the task of completing it themselves, or reassign the work to a different person. If the project has been passed along to many different people, it may be given back to the person who was first assigned to it. This will happen only if the Producer is convinced that the first person will not only handle it better when armed with clearer instructions, but will also complete it on time—and correctly.

3. Withhold

Often, Producers in distress will pull everything in closer to themselves and not let anyone else be a part of a project. In their frustration, they aren't sure if others can or will successfully and correctly manage their assignments. As a result, Producers will double up their own workloads and pull the tasks into their realm of duties until they're satisfied that others are capable of handling the work in a timely manner, with excellence.

If not convinced of this, Producers may even withhold future assignments until they believe others can be trusted with them. Because Producers are such gracious people, an action of this magnitude is seldom done in a state of anger or as a "group" punishment. Excellence is important to Producers and they expect others to accomplish their part of *any assignment* in the best, most efficient, and timely manner possible.

If you are a Producer and feel yourself exhibiting these distress flares, you must catch yourself and bring them under control as quickly as possible. If you know a Producer who is in distress, stop what you are doing immediately and make the time to express genuine gratitude for all that they do, with sincere and thoughtful words of caring and appreciation.

LEADERSHIP STYLES

Producers are resourceful, genial leaders who ensure the best use of all available resources, utilizing a close management style, focused through two or three key people.

- Gracious

- Thoughtful

- Insightful

- Pursue excellence

- See people as valuable resources

- Are able to demonstrate the best use of resources to accomplish goals

- Are good money managers

OTHER LEADERSHIP TRAITS

A cultural philosophy of Producers: "By investing our resources and directing our efforts, we will add value to our organization. Then we and our organization will be successful."

A Producer organizational structure: Micro-management

When in health, the Producer leader will empower others.

When in distress, the Producer leader may become a selfish controller.

POSSIBLE PROFESSIONS

Producers can easily serve as a chief financial officer or a chief executive officer, financial planner, stock broker, banker, department head, or administrator. They can work in the hospitality industry, restaurant industry, materials management, or inventory control—in any function that creates abundance and wealth.

CLUES FOR COMMUNICATING

The following clues are helpful when communicating with a Producer:

+ *Verbal clues*: The Producer will be gracious, offering coffee and other refreshments. Listen for words that show thoughtfulness, hospitality, or resource management. Producers will want to know the cost of products or whether an investment is a wise use of the company's resources.

+ *Non-verbal clues*: Producers will intentionally make you feel special.

+ *Visual clues*: The Producer's office is warm, inviting, and orderly. One or two candy bowls will be available for visitors and coworkers. The Producer tends to dress in a professional manner with conservative elegance.

+ *Affirmation phrases*: Show a Producer a genuine appreciation for the time they are giving you. Congratulate them for the care they give customers or their staff's hospitality. Producers need appreciation. If you work for a Producer, let them know you want to be a good resource.

+ *Behavior that can frustrate a Producer*: Playing your cards too close to the chest and not sharing information, such as bottom-line item costs or expenses. Having an attitude that cost doesn't matter. Being ungrateful or unappreciative.

+ *Ways to motivate a Producer*: Intentionally show the value behind the cost and carefully consider the Producer's time and input. They tend to be a valuable resource so don't be afraid to ask for their advice or seek their knowledge.

Producers need appreciation and like giving quality gifts or having quality resources. Don't consider cutting corners by using cheaper products or services. Producers are pleased when you acknowledge their thoughtfulness and value. When appropriate, give them a thoughtful, quality gift.

EXAMPLE OF A FAMOUS PRODUCER

We should all do something to right the wrongs that we see and not just complain about them.

—Jacqueline "Jackie" Kennedy Onassis[16]

John F. Kennedy was assassinated less than three years into his presidency. Five years later, his widow married Greek shipping magnate Aristotle Onassis. But the elegant, cultured "Jackie O" was much more than someone's wife or widow.

Jackie read dozens of books before she even started school. She won several national equestrian championships. After college, she worked as a photojournalist, asking topical or

16. Amy Higley, "5 Life Lessons from Jackie Kennedy," *FaithCounts*, December 19, 2016 (faithcounts.com/5-life-lessons-jackie-kennedy).

personal questions such as, "What is your candid opinion of marriage?"[17]

She never wanted to be called "First Lady," saying it sounded like a horse's name. Producers are all about excellence and seeing the White House's dismal, bland furnishings left her so aghast that she led the project to replace them with beautiful, historic pieces. It was, she said, "a question of scholarship." Jackie also displayed a high Producer's spirit of gracious hospitality.

Later, she worked as a book editor for nearly twenty years.[18] She spent four years pursuing Michael Jackson to persuade him to write his autobiography, *Moonwalk*. She acquired and edited nearly a hundred works, including *Allure* by Diana Vreeland and *The Power of Myth* by Joseph Campbell.

Although Jackie was married to two powerful, wealthy men, she was known as a good manager of her own life, finances, and resources. She did not surround herself with glitz and glamour, but with taste and quality befitting a life of quiet elegance.

Producers do not impulsively give to every cause, but take quiet action when one catches their attention. Jackie worked tirelessly to save landmarks such as New York City's Grand Central Terminal, which was threatened for destruction under a redevelopment plan.

The only routine with me is no routine at all.

—Jackie Kennedy Onassis

17. Malea Walker, "Jackie Kennedy: Inquiring Camera Girl," May 22, 2018, https://blogs.loc.gov/headlinesandheroes.

18. Nancy Bilyeau, "Jackie Kennedy's Third Act: How the twice-widowed American icon became a successful book editor—at $200 a week," *Town & Country* magazine, August 18, 2017.

NOTES

10

CONTEMPLATOR:
QUESTING FOR KNOWLEDGE

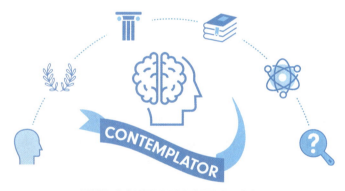

THE CONTEMPLATOR ICON

All of the elements of the original icon harken to the Contemplator's highly cognitive approach to life. It includes *The Thinker*, of course, as well as books atop a pillar and olive branches to denote the Contemplator's peaceful nature.

With the overarching tendency of Contemplators to think and think, and then think some more, the new icon features the cognitive intelligence category head with a drawing of a brain.

After reflecting seriously and in-depth about a particular subject for a long period of time, the Contemplator may not even wish to discuss or share any of the thought-out conclusions they have just reached. The gaining of knowledge is not a way for a Contemplator to impress others with their scholarly skills. Instead, they derive satisfaction from *knowing*.

They never feel obligated to share their knowledge, nor do they usually feel it's important to so. This might seem selfish, but in the mind of the Contemplator, they are merely trying to fulfill their own personal desire to acquire knowledge for the sheer joy of learning.

More than anything, the Contemplator desires to learn, study, and be a life-long seeker of knowledge and wisdom.

Although Contemplators don't necessarily desire to be peace-keepers, they are committed to personal, internal peace. If they are in a situation with high or ongoing conflict, they will, in many cases, just leave. If they can't do so, they may seem to zone out. Contemplators prefer low-conflict environments filled with pleasant, peaceful relationships. They don't do well in hostile situations.

Contemplators typically have brilliant minds and high IQs, yet they often don't reach their full potential until later in life, when they soar upward.

THE CONTEMPLATOR INTELLIGENCE: ANALYTICAL-COGNITIVE

Contemplators usually have so many interests that it's difficult for them to stay focused on one single agenda to achieve professional and personal success. Some have been known to go to college for ten years and yet never settle on a major.

Contemplators are interested many professions, including languages, music, photography, graphic arts, math, or computer programming—their list of interests could go on indefinitely and include anything that involves using their minds. They are rarely interested in work that involves using their hands unless they have a high score in the Doer Life Language as well.

Once they do determine what they want to do, they definitely have what it takes to reach new heights in their chosen field. As unusually brilliant scholars by nature, they often have many advanced degrees in more than one field.

CONTEMPLATOR SYMBOL FROM NATURE

For centuries, owls have symbolized wisdom and intelligence. Owls seem to be calm, tranquil, and solitary, much like the Contemplator. They survey their surroundings from high and lofty places; Contemplators generally are intellectually higher and loftier than most.

Like owls, Contemplators are often nocturnal, staying up late to study and think. Owls usually live alone or in pairs. Similarly, Contemplators tend to avoid crowds and large groups.

CONTEMPLATOR COLOR

The color blue makes us think of clear skies and clean, deep mountain lakes. Blue is calming, peaceful, and still. Contemplators are cool and calm under pressure and prefer conflict-free environments. Blue signifies the Contemplator's intelligence, wisdom, spirituality, sensitivity, solitude, and tranquility.

As complex human beings, Contemplators may desire solitude and contentment, but they don't want a life of emptiness or complete separation from the world.

> As you listen to the intertwining rhythms of life around you, be sure to keep a fine-tuned ear for the counter-beat that Contemplators add to the symphony. They do march to a different drummer, but that beat is the steady, calming, consistent beat that adds peace and contentment to life. Celebrate Contemplators and their deep and gentle influence on our world.
>
> —Anna Kendall

POSITIVE CHARACTERISTICS OR ATTRIBUTES OF CONTEMPLATORS

14% Those with Contemplator as their first or primary language will have most or many of the following characteristics. Those with Contemplator as their second or third language, and so on, will have fewer of these characteristics. *For more detail, see Appendix G.*

Cautious	Complex thinkers	Need alone time
Seek contentment	Quiet	Not easily controlled
Exhibit deference	Private	Deep thinkers
Determined	Have well-defined boundaries	Validate truth
Loyal	Guard their time	Research facts
Visibly unresponsive	Unusual sense of humor	Think before speaking
Dislike change	Verbal when interested	Higher IQ
Not very sensitive	Calm	Avoid conflict
Need private space	Comfortable with silence	Philosophical & studious
Have many interests	Life-long learners	Analytical

Approximately 14 percent of the population speak Contemplator as their primary Life Language.

Any Life Language can have a high or even genius IQ. However, we have observed that more Contemplators have higher-than-average IQs. They are often members of Mensa.   —Anna Kendall

FOUR KEYS TO SUCCESSFUL COMMUNICATION

1. Answer Their Filter Question: *"Am I Interested in This?"*

This is how Contemplators view (and screen) the outside world's communication. If Contemplators are not personally interested in what's being said, they may just switch off the conversation. They seem to literally disappear right in front of you. There's often no response from a Contemplator, either verbally or visually, when they elect to disappear.

People who work with Contemplators on a daily basis often tell us something along these lines: "There are times when I want to take my closed hand and knock him on his forehead and ask, 'Hello, hello? Is anyone home?'"

Mature Contemplator communicators can decide to focus on what is being discussed and express polite interest as a way to stay connected with a group and show that they care or are intentionally present.

2. Meet Their Need From Others: *Personal Space*

Contemplators generally do not compete for the "floor" in meetings where numerous people are talking. They chose to sit quietly. The Contemplator may have the answers you are looking for, but they won't compete with others to *tell* you. Because of their private nature, Contemplators need to be asked what they think.

Some individuals get energized by being around a group of people. Contemplators tend to feel drained. At some point, they need personal space and *time alone* to get re-energized. After that, they can return to interact.

3. Encourage Their Passion: *to Know*

Contemplators are generally lifelong students. Many earn advanced degrees, continuing to go college for many years. They are not there just to earn a degree, but because there's so much to learn! Contemplators often spend their entire lifetime being in a continual state of learning. They often follow their intellectual interests rather than following their major career path. Their ability to study and learn *knowledge* makes them a valuable addition to any team.

4. Validate Their Character: *Loyalty*

Contemplators have great loyalty to the past and the present. For example, if their family had a certain breed of dog as pets when they were children, they would feel disloyal if they got a different breed. There's some degree of nostalgia involved.

Contemplators feel a deep loyalty to their current friends, employers, and old friends they may not have seen for years, but who, nevertheless, they continue to feel close to. Loyalty is a very powerful character strength and Contemplators are brilliant, quiet, and loyal.

ESSENTIAL TRAIT TO CULTIVATE: CONNECTEDNESS

Contemplators can appear quite self-sufficient, existing without appearing to have many close relationships. Their interests are so varied that they don't need outsiders to be entertained. They find ways to entertain themselves that usually involve scholarly activities that let them continue to learn and grow. They may not even realize they are not connecting with others.

But to be successful, Contemplators must learn to connect, communicate, and develop socially and professionally. In most cases, once they discover their importance to others, Contemplators are usually quite capable of making connections and conversing.

SUCCESS HABIT TO DEVELOP: CLOSE THE GAP BETWEEN THINKING, FEELING, AND ACTING

Contemplators like to think, gather facts, consider, reason, analyze, and *then think some more*. As they are thinking, they usually are *not* talking. To lessen these communication gaps, it would be appropriate for Contemplators to discuss some of their thoughts so others don't feel left out.

To be a Healthy Contemplator, they must look for ways to acknowledge the feelings of others. Contemplators do feel, but very deeply and quietly. Sometimes people misinterpret their body language as being tuned out and disinterested.

> The soul enjoys silence and peace, not by many reasonings, but rather by simply contemplating the truth.
> —Peter of Alcantara, Spanish Franciscan friar

CONTEMPLATOR CASE STUDY

Matthew teaches information technology and is considered an outstanding professor. His classes are always full; his students find his lessons to be fact-filled but sprinkled with point- making humor. While at his podium, Matthew is quite comfortable, personable, and even extroverted. But back in his office, he is quiet, doesn't like to see many people, and really dreads faculty meetings or any social events. He's not comfortable with small talk or meeting new people.

Matthew's bride was confused by the dichotomy between his professional, on-stage persona and his quiet personality at home, where he seemed to prefer silence to talking. She didn't understand why Matthew prefers one-on-one relationships, just them and another couple, rather than a room full of people.

As a wedding gift, another faculty member paid for Kendall Life Languages Profiles for Matthew and his bride, as well as a meeting with a Life Languages certified coach. The newlyweds were amazed by their KLLP findings. They told us, "Reading our individual KLLP portraits was amazing, a total *aha* learning moment for both of us!"

At Life Languages International, we have discovered that most of the time, when people are getting to know each other and falling in love, they are multi-lingual—they express the other person's primary language. But six months into their marriage, they look at each other and wonder, *What happened? You used to like what I like and now you don't.* That's where Matthew and his wife had found themselves.

Once she understood where Matthew was coming from as a high Contemplator, their difficulties disappeared. They learned how to communicate with one another, by speaking the appropriate Life Languages, meeting each other's needs, and knowing how to respond to any distress flares.

At work, Matthew talked openly about his KLLP and the entire department profited by becoming aware of Matthew's thought processes. The other professors even laughed at some of the preconceived judgments they had made about him and the resulting misunderstandings.

Most importantly, Matthew's marriage is stronger than ever.

> For many Contemplators, activities and talking can go on for too long, thereby draining them of energy and health. Like a run-down battery, Contemplators must then set aside some time to be alone and recharge.
>
> —Anna Kendall

DISTRESS FLARES: JAW

1. **Justify**: "Well, the reason I did that was because….!"

The Contemplator who's feeling backed into a corner will try to justify their behavior rather than acknowledging, "I didn't do the task. I'm sorry. I will do it now." Often, it's an *issue of pride* that Contemplators fall back on. They are totally capable and generally brilliant and can easily complete any assignment given to them. After they justify their actions or reasons, they may move into the second flare.

2. **Accuse**: "You didn't make your directions clear" or "You didn't finish your part first, so I *couldn't do mine*."

Contemplators may redirect the blame away from themselves and onto someone else, thereby excusing themselves of any responsibility.

3. **Withdraw:** "If I'm not appreciated or valued, I will just leave!"

This kind of prideful remark could be referring to an ongoing meeting or might have stronger implications, such as actually quitting their job. However, under normal circumstances such as staff meetings, Contemplators don't go into the third distress flare in an obvious manner; instead, they may emotionally, mentally, or physically withdraw.

While Contemplators enjoy undivided attention and quality time, they need personal space. When they are around too many people for too long, they can go into distress. An observant friend or coworker who recognizes these distress signals can help a Contemplator find a quiet location to think in peace.

CASE STUDY: MANAGER GIVEN TIME TO THINK

I have made it a priority to study the Life Languages communication portrait of all of my executives. I have a plant manager who is a very high Responder/ Contemplator. She is one of the best employees I have ever had on my team, so every morning, we have a "feel good" meeting... followed by a list of things I want her to comment on, as well as offer any suggestion she thinks would be productive for plant operations.

I have discovered that if I give her the time she needs to process the topics we covered in our meetings, even if it is uncomfortable and I have to wait, sometimes for several days, what she comes up with for solutions are consistently brilliant.

I am a firm believer that learning the communication portrait of your team will lead to immeasurable success in the workplace.

—John Paty, Owner, Paty Preferred Meat Co.

Dallas, TX

LEADERSHIP STYLES

+ Usually brilliant and have a high IQ

+ Do not feel compelled to talk

+ Usually share knowledge after giving topic or problem serious thought and having conducted thorough research

+ Have the ability to care deeply, although generally quietly

+ Loyal to those they lead

+ Private by nature

+ Verbal when interested or when teaching or leading

+ Quiet socially

+ Expect others to handle their particular area of responsibility

+ Project a peaceful leadership manner and work atmosphere

Contemplators are quiet, peaceful leaders who impart wisdom, maturity, and skill to others. They seek deeper truths, facts, or information. Contemplators validate direction, expecting others to do their own work and giving them the autonomy to do so.

OTHER LEADERSHIP TRAITS

A cultural philosophy of Contemplators: "By working independently and sharing as we go along, we will continue to get better and achieve more."

A Contemplator organizational structure: Unified Autonomy

When in health, the Contemplator is a sensitive, intellectual, and thoughtful leader.

When in distress, the Contemplator leader may become insensitive, unilateral, and passive-aggressive.

POSSIBLE PROFESSIONS

Contemplators can be musicians, mathematicians, software developers, draftsmen, engineers, linguists, college professors, doctors, scientists, researchers, photographers, forest rangers, librarians, postal carriers, writers, pilots, actors, and lawyers.

Contemplators tend to prefer a private lifestyle. They prefer peace and quiet rather than noise, confusion, and hordes of people or large meetings. They like to avoid large crowds and prefer one-on-one relationships, where they can express their deep thoughts and be heard above the roar of a crowd.   —Anna Kendall

CLUES FOR COMMUNICATING

The following clues are helpful when communicating with a Contemplator:

+ *Verbal clues*: Listen for thinking and reflective words. "Let me think about this and get back to you..." or "I will research and look into this." There may be long pauses in the conversation when they are talking to you.

+ *Non-verbal clues*: Contemplators like to maintain a wide personal space around themselves when conversing. They may occasionally have a blank stare like "an absent-minded professor." Contemplators usually have one or more college degrees.

+ *Visual clues*: There is abundant intellectual stimulation in their office and home on many and varied subjects. Their spaces are usually interesting. There's likely to be clutter, art works, items related to languages, antiques, and numerous obscure items. Contemplators typically dress casually and the men often have facial hair.

+ *Affirmation phrases*: Give them your undivided attention and don't move too closely into their personal space. Use opening, questioning sentences such as, "What are your thoughts?" "Have you considered...?" and "I brought some research that I'd like your opinion on." Allow silence. If a Contemplator pauses, let them think for as long as necessary. Remember, most Contemplators take time to think and sometimes rethink. Be patient!

+ *Behavior that can frustrate a Contemplator*: Pushing them for immediate action or an immediate decision;

not respecting their need for space, alone-time, or silence; too much chit-chat about subjects they are not interested in; hinting that they don't understand how *you* feel; challenging their intelligence; questioning their way of doing things; or not understanding a conclusion they've made. Contemplators have difficulty handling criticism, chaos, confusion, or too much noise.

+ *Ways to motivate a Contemplator*: Compliment their reasoning or analytical abilities. Express interest in their logical and well-thought-out answers. Tell them, "Let me give you some time to consider this" and "What more would you like for me to provide for you?" Don't push for decisions—give them time. They may be resistant to change. Make them comfortable by mirroring their posture and stance.

EXAMPLE OF A FAMOUS CONTEMPLATOR

I have no special talents. I am only passionately curious.   —Albert Einstein[19]

Generally, when Contemplators have time alone, their cognitive brilliance and creativity come up with amazing insights or discoveries. Scientist and mathematician Albert Einstein is best known for his equation $E=mc^2$ (energy equals mass times the speed of light squared) and his general theory of relativity, which explains that what we perceive as gravity arises from the curvature of space and time.

Given a compass at age five, he marveled at the way it constantly pointed in one direction, no matter what he did. That

19. *The Collected Papers of Albert Einstein*, Princeton University Press (einsteinpapers.press.princeton.edu).

awakened his life-long passion for learning—a Contemplator trait.

Einstein's clothing was often rumpled and his wild mane of white hair made him look like a "mad scientist." He never wore socks, he explained, because his long big toes eventually wore holes in them. Contemplators "march to a different drummer" and this definitely applies to clothing choices. Women who are high Contemplators may not even have an awareness of fashion or the desire to keep up with it. They may also wear little or no makeup or keep their hair in any style.

Einstein had a wonderful sense of humor. Once, when asked to explain the theory of relativity, he said, "Put your hand on a hot stove for a minute, and it seems like an hour. Sit with a pretty girl for an hour, and it seems like a minute. That's relativity!"[20]

In his essay, *Notes for an Autobiography*, published in *The Saturday Review* in November 1949, Einstein wrote:

> For me it is not dubious that our thinking goes on for the most part without use of signs (words) and beyond that to a considerable degree unconsciously. For how, otherwise, should it happen that sometimes we "wonder" quite spontaneously about some experience? This "wondering" seems to occur when an experience comes into conflict with a world of concepts which is already sufficiently fixed in us. Whenever such a conflict is experienced hard and intensively it reacts back upon our thought world in a decisive way.

20. The Albert Einstein Website Online (www.alberteinsteinsite.com).

NOTES

THE KEY TO SUCCESSFUL COMMUNICATION WITH THE KENDALL LIFE LANGUAGES™

ANSWER THE FILTER—MEET THE NEED—
ENCOURAGE THE PASSION—
VALIDATE THE CHARACTER

	Mover	Doer	Influencer
Major Characteristics	Innovative Direct High Standards	Practical Diligent Detailed	Intuitive Inclusive Enthusiastic
Filter Question	"What's your motive?"	"Are you doing your share?"	"Are we communicating?"
Need From Others	Action & Congruency	Action & Appreciation	Affirmation & Connectedness
Driving Passion	To Innovate	To Finish	To Encourage
Key Character Strength	Courage	Trustworthiness	Enthusiasm
Distress Flares	**ADA:** Attack, Demand, Attack	**MAG:** Martyred, Accuse, Grumble	**DAE:** Deny, Argue, Escape
If we remain in "Distress Flares" without moving back into healthy communication, we may descend into further distress.			
Essential Qualities to be Developed	Maintenance	Delegate	Integrity to their word
	Spirit of Finisher	Look Ahead	Active Listening

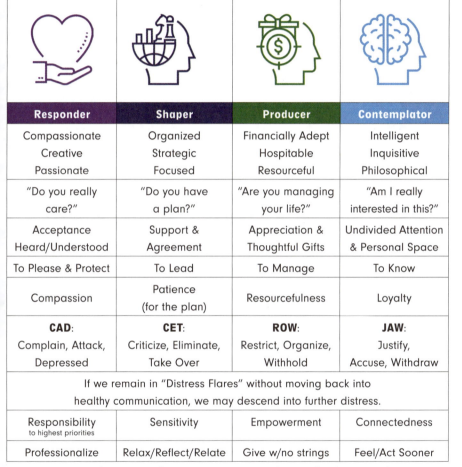

Responder	Shaper	Producer	Contemplator
Compassionate Creative Passionate	Organized Strategic Focused	Financially Adept Hospitable Resourceful	Intelligent Inquisitive Philosophical
"Do you really care?"	"Do you have a plan?"	"Are you managing your life?"	"Am I really interested in this?"
Acceptance Heard/Understood	Support & Agreement	Appreciation & Thoughtful Gifts	Undivided Attention & Personal Space
To Please & Protect	To Lead	To Manage	To Know
Compassion	Patience (for the plan)	Resourcefulness	Loyalty
CAD: Complain, Attack, Depressed	**CET**: Criticize, Eliminate, Take Over	**ROW**: Restrict, Organize, Withhold	**JAW**: Justify, Accuse, Withdraw
If we remain in "Distress Flares" without moving back into healthy communication, we may descend into further distress.			
Responsibility to highest priorities	Sensitivity	Empowerment	Connectedness
Professionalize	Relax/Reflect/Relate	Give w/no strings	Feel/Act Sooner

PART THREE:

USING THE KLLP

11

CORPORATE COMMUNICATION

The 7 Life Languages program is so simple, a young adult could master it, yet it's also so deep, it can take up to two or three years for it to become part of a corporate culture. When people truly understand one another, the positive results can be endless. We have seen how Life Languages International's training of *Communication IQ*, both online and on-site, has rippled to strengthen relationships not only in companies but also in personal lives. We've been thrilled to train and certify Life Languages coaches to help us build communication bridges around the world.

AN HR DIRECTOR'S TESTIMONY

Amanda, a human resources director, told us:

"We had a conflict between two coworkers on the same team. Their disagreement had grown large enough that it was impacting their relationship on a personal level. Fortunately, both individuals had recently taken the Life Languages profile and it was the perfect instrument for helping them navigate through the conflict. Upon reviewing their profiles, they truly had an aha moment. It helped them better understand *why* they responded the way they did to each other and the situation. This self-realization and enlightenment forced these individuals to assume ownership for their parts in the conflict. Amazingly, this all happened even before I ever brought the two together to seek a positive conclusion.

"When I met with the two of them together, we walked through each of their profiles. I can't tell you how helpful this 'walk' was! Both parties were able to better see not only *why they responded* the way that they did but were also able to better understand why their coworker responded the way he did. Not only had they each taken ownership of their own actions in the conflict, they also both had found a deeper understanding of their teammate that had never existed before. By the time we had completed the meeting, they were shaking hands, laughing, and discussing having some fun outside of work.

"I can't say enough what a priceless tool the Life Languages Profile has been to our workplace. I highly recommend any business make it a part of their employee development process!"

THE HIGH COST OF POOR COMMUNICATION

Poor communication costs an organization time and money, both immediately and in the long-term. Misunderstandings delay projects, reduce productivity, and cause needless stress and tension among coworkers. Even if both parties in a workplace conflict want to move past their disagreement, it can spill over into their future interactions. It can also affect others in the organization.

Learning the communication styles of the 7 Life Languages does more than just teach people how to communicate. It teaches them how to think differently, control emotions, better structure action, handle conflict, build effective teams, and give direction to strategic leadership development.

BENEFITS IN A NUTSHELL

+ **Mutual understanding**. Effective communication provides both management and employees with clarity. When an employee can accurately communicate what he's thinking or feeling, management can better anticipate and fulfill the employee's needs. The same applies to client relationships. Employees who can communicate more effectively with customers will find it easier to work with them, including those who are upset or hostile.

✦ **Less drama and conflict.** Employees who are trained in the Life Languages find it easier to understand each other and thus experience less workplace tension. Disagreements can be resolved more readily because each person knows the other's point of view. There are fewer misunderstandings, arguments, and feelings of frustration.

✦ **Better customer and employee retention rates.** Giving customers and employees the right amount of attention begins with skilled communication. Dissatisfied employees and customers who feel like they're *just a number* tend not to stay with an organization for very long.

A 2018 Gallup poll found that only 12 percent of employees, regardless of the industry, strongly agree that their organization does a great job onboarding new employees.[21] The failure to help a new hire acclimate to a company and its products or services can prevent that person from forming a strong bond with the employer. It's no wonder, then, that as many as 50 percent of employees leave within the first eighteen months of employment, according to the Society for Human Resource Management. That kind of turnover can affect your bottom line and contribute to morale problems among existing staff.

Every employer's greatest challenge is to understand how to communicate to their talented employees and keep them engaged and motivated for long-term employment. We have written this book to help organizations prepare strategies to keep their staff connected and committed.

---

21. https://news.gallup.com/opinion/gallup/234419/why-onboarding-experience-key-retention.aspx (accessed Sept. 12, 2018)

"In the corporate community, communication between executives, employees, customers, and clients is
the very 'air' that creates productivity. When it's not
well-defined or understood, the 'air' becomes stale,
unhealthy, toxic, and chaotic. This kind of corporate
culture makes everyone sweat, from the board room to
the break room. But when the air is filtered through
mutual, positive, character-based communication, everyone breathes easier because they understand each
other's languages. The culture becomes inspirational
rather than combative. Differences are depersonalized
through our self-reporting communication assessment,
which has a 92 to 98 percent reporting accuracy over the
past twenty-five years. That says something! It removes
all the guesswork on how to manage people well and develop them strategically. It empowers you to deal with every individual on your team based on what and how they
need communication from you. Likewise, it empowers
your team to know you and what and how they need to
respond to you. On every level, it's a win-win for everyone!"   —Gerald Parsons, Chief Operating Officer
Life Languages International

Whether you are starting your own business or joining a
new company, an established supervisor or a corporate officer,
the 7 Life Languages communication styles will increase your
success on all levels. Once people reach the C-Suite, technical or functional expertise and business fundamentals matter

less than do leadership skills, including the ability to effectively communicate and articulate vision.

JOB SWAP CASE STUDY

We were working with a law enforcement agency and the sheriff asked us to conduct a workshop for all of his seconds in command, who were chiefs of various departments. Halfway through the day, after going over each person's KLLP, the five men and one woman became very verbally transparent, which is rather unusual for law enforcement officers.

The female chief said, "Well, if we're being really honest, I don't think all of my duty assignments utilize my greatest strengths." She handled most of the public relations duties and had to personally give speeches and attend numerous public activities, from business grand openings to ribbon-cuttings. Additionally, this first language Mover was often pulled in to interview victims and their families.

"I agree with her," another chief said. "After reading my profile, I also don't think all my duty assignments are fully in line with my strengths. I've wanted to talk about it for a long time but didn't know how." He was head of the Special Weapons and Tactics (SWAT) team—and his first language was Influencer. This chief told us that in his spare time, he was involved in several community organizations and was often called on to give motivational talks, especially in schools.

The sheriff, who was also a first language Mover, looked at them, looked at us, and then said, "Do you two want to switch jobs?"

They both jumped at the opportunity. So they set a time to explore the departmental changes.

The sheriff had believed that the female chief would be better with victims and public relations. But the truth was, she had always wanted to head up SWAT—and she had the Life Language skills and ability to potentially do a great job. The male chief could certainly handle the SWAT division, but his heart was in relationships. He loved to interact with the public because his preferred communication style was Influencer.

Everything worked out and we have continued to serve this organization.

KEY TAKE-AWAY

The right people in the right jobs are critical to an organization's success or a company's bottom line profits. An individual doesn't have to be holding down a senior management position or earning a six-figure salary to have an impact. Upper management might not even know the names of the people who are out in the field, yet they can be key to the company's health and efficiency.

One of the best ways to make sure people are in the right jobs is to discover their communication styles. Otherwise, how would you know that a Responder, for instance, should not be stuck in a cubical? Or why a Mover might be frustrated by a repetitive job that doesn't require a lot of action?

KLLP AND A CITY GOVERNMENT

Often, relationship problems in the workplace are passed off as gender, race, or age discrimination when the problem is usually a communication issue. Here is an example:

Several years ago, Life Languages International called on a city in Texas. During our presentation, a human resources director unexpectedly interrupted us.

"Thank you, but the city is not interested in your program," she said.

End of story...or so we thought. As we were closing our briefcases and preparing to leave, the director suddenly spoke up.

"I want to tell you about my relationship with my boss and see if you have any ideas or suggestions," she said. Obviously frustrated, she told us her boss was a quiet man and made decisions slowly, making sure that he had *all* the facts first. She told us he also didn't like interruptions and tended to keep his office door closed. Finally, the director told us that she thought her boss simply didn't like her.

"This is the best job I have ever had," she said. "But I'm so stressed over not feeling accepted and appreciated that I'm seriously thinking of leaving." She wondered whether the problem was an "age thing" or a racial issue. "I'm just not sure. The only thing I think I know is that I'm older than he is." The director ended her story by telling us that she had thought of every possible solution but nothing had worked.

After listening to the director's very personal story, it was clear that she and her boss had a serious but fixable language issue. We gave her a plan that she agreed to strictly follow for the next two weeks:

- Rather than interrupt him by knocking on his door or calling him several times a day, wait till the end of each day. Prepare a list of events and messages that specifically involved him, would be of interest to him, or needed his attention, all in bullet points.
- Make a highlighted notation on anything that required a decision the next day to give him the opportunity to process the problem overnight and reach a solution.
- Screen all incoming phone calls and keep a log of them so he could choose which ones to return—and when.
- Allow no interruptions during the day, for any reason, unless it was absolutely urgent or he requested it.
- Always begin any verbal communication with the following statement, "I'll give you some time to process 'this'...and if you want me to do something, please let me know."

At the end of first week, the director called us.

"You will not believe what has happened," she said. "My boss came to my desk today and said, 'You know, I think we are finally really getting in sync and starting to work well together.' It was truly a wonderful moment for me!"

Because of this interaction plan we suggested to the director, we've had the city as a client for almost eighteen years.

We have profiled all city employees, including fire and police personnel, and we're called in occasionally as consultants. The director and her boss have frequently attended our certified training classes and shared their experience. We have had numerous referrals from them, enabling us to help other city governments.

CASE STUDY: A RESPONDER-DOER

When we were in the psychiatric hospital business, we had an invaluable office manager whose second communication style impacted her first. A high Responder, Sue was wonderful working with patients and their families. She genuinely cared for and understood the internal, emotional pain and suffering the patient was experiencing. Sue nurtured and listened to every patient and continued to stay involved with them until they were placed with a therapist or treatment plan that *she knew* would give them the help they needed.

Sue's second Life Language was Doer, so she was diligent, dedicated, and responsible. She always finished *everything* she started. She would not leave for the day until all of the insurance, medical, and government paperwork was completed accurately. Yet she would set this part of her job aside to address (with genuine care) the pain of any individual who came into the office. Sue was not a professional counselor, yet she exhibited so much love and concern that the person in crisis was soothed even before they met a counselor or were admitted for treatment. Her compassion was so great, that in many cases, she helped to start the patient's healing process.

AN ASSIST THAT BACKFIRED

One day, during Sue's lunch break, Fred decided to "help" her. He recalls:

I looked at Sue's office and decided I knew a better physical arrangement that would help her be more comfortable and efficient. As a high Mover, I tend to always see a better way of doing things and am never satisfied with the status quo. I quickly re-arranged everything in her office. When she got back, I expected her to be excited about my hard work and how I had made her office so much more efficient! Now, thanks to all my creative effort, it was much easier for her to access each and every area.

But upon her return, rather than being excited, Sue was quiet. Because we were extremely busy that afternoon, I didn't think much about what seemed like her unusual mood swing. At the end of the day, Sue came to me and very sadly asked if I wanted her resignation. I was totally shocked.

"What are you talking about? You are great at your job!" I told her.

"Well, you must not be pleased with my work because you totally rearranged my office. I thought you were preparing it for someone else. Since you moved everything around, I thought you weren't satisfied with the way I'm running things."

People who have Responder as their primary Life Language tend to take things personally because they live with their heart and soul engaged to please and protect.

I told her, "Sue, just watch how fast I put things back the way you had them! I promise, your office will be restored exactly back to the way it was—right down to the last paper clip."

Later, we laughed about how people speaking the Mover and Responder/Doer combinations can work together, but also unknowingly sabotage their relationship. Just because Movers have ideas they think are great doesn't mean others agree with them. We are all in the process of growing. Sometimes, it's best not to mess with perfection!

12

THE LIFE LANGUAGES' "POWER TWINS"

In a world of compromise, confusion, and chaos, we need men and women of character everywhere, especially in the workforce.

As you study the 7 Life Languages, you notice that each is made up of "character qualities." You probably already possess and demonstrate the qualities of your top language indicated by your Life Language Assessment. If not, with sincere effort, these characteristics are attainable and can become a part of you.

However, learning your primary Life Language or discovering your KLLP—which shows all seven communication styles, from your strongest to weakest—doesn't mean you should ignore the others' positive traits. Exploring and learning to speak all seven Life Languages as they are needed will help you grow in character while you become a more skillful communicator.

The more these communication styles are internalized, the kinder we become in our interactions.

People who deliberately attempt to use the character traits to manipulate or coerce others—for instance, telling a Mover it's fine if they don't finish a task to make them beholden to you—goes against the spirit of what we've set out to accomplish. We don't want anyone to use the Life Languages in that manner.

THE NEED TO DEVELOP CHARACTER

To be successful in life, you need the power twins that come from the 7 Life Languages: fluent communication and healthy character. If you examine the reasons why employees are terminated, it boils down to flaws in their character, communication...or both.

As we watch the daily barrage of news and social media, it appears that too many people lack good character. Insults and crude, rude behavior are often the norm. Imagine what this is doing to our world and our children. The more we observe the behavior of so many, the more it becomes obvious that they're stuck waving their distress flares. They lack integrity.

When a building is strong and sound, we say it has structural integrity. It can withstand an earthquake. The word *integrity* originates from the Latin root word *intact*, which basically means the ability to hold up under enormous stress.

Some people are unable to effectively remain *intact* when there's a crisis in their lives. The storm buffets against them and they almost immediately collapse, often in their family or career. They seem to be unaware of the underlying problem until the crisis hits.

"Normal" doesn't test your integrity, but a crisis does. By the time a business is hit by a crisis, it's often too late to fix what's wrong. The damage was ongoing and happening in real-time.

IF SOMEONE LACKS CHARACTER

Here are some indications that someone lacks character:

1. **Self-Absorbed, Self-Centered, or Selfish.** This type of individual will harm an organization as well as their family and friends. Life is all about them. When we hear of someone who "won't go the distance," it's usually referring to a person who has a reputation for being unreliable, someone you can't trust. A self-centered, self-absorbed person is rarely an effective team player. When carried to an extreme, they may become narcissistic. People like this will probably never experience real and true personal success. People of character don't continually put their own needs above others in a business or family.

2. **Self-Worth Is Determined by Others.** A *secure* person with character can see the "right way" and lead people through a tough situation. An insecure leader, or one who lacks character, will bend with every change in public opinion, ultimately causing more

problems. These people may be somewhat codependent.

3. **Keeping Secrets.** We are as unhealthy as the secrets we keep. We shouldn't tell everyone everything about us, but we should share anything that's bothering us with someone we trust who cares about us. We are not referring only to current, day-to-day secrets, but also secrets that may date back to childhood that still make us feel shame or guilt. Such secrets are like a hundred-pound load that can't be put down. It takes a lot of energy to carry that load—energy that could be used to live in the freedom and fullness of now.

4. **Failure to Keep Our Word.** This isn't just about keeping promises; it's about always doing what we say we're going to do. It's better to say nothing and surprise everyone by delivering than blurting out an intention we know we can't fulfill. People lose confidence and trust in us when we constantly take on assignments that we don't complete. Saying we will do something and then not following through is immature and displays a lack of character.

5. **Too Many Compromises.** Leadership is not about getting everyone to like us or finding the easiest path. It's about finding the best way forward, even when our decision doesn't have the approval of others. If we make too many compromises in business or our personal life, we are bound to be ineffective. Compromises also show a lack of character and commitment.

However, we *can* seek wise counsel on major decisions.

6. **Refuse Appropriate Correction.** No one likes to be corrected; it may seem like criticism, which can make us defensive. We may deny that we're wrong. But if we make a conscious decision to listen to the correction, consider it, and appreciate the person giving it, we will be displaying good character and humility. It's okay to say, "Let me think about this" or "I would like to process this idea." After we openly evaluate the correction, if we choose to make the suggested change, we show character by thanking the other person.

7. **Consistently Seek Personal Recognition.** We all know people who continuously say "I" rather than "we," even when there's a team or departmental accomplishment for which praise and recognition should be shared. Soon, the team energy is depleted and the individuals who were ignored feel devalued.

PROBLEMS *WILL* COME

It's impossible for anyone to go through life without problems. However, when you intentionally strive to develop excellent character qualities, you can face any professional or personal issues head-on.

We've seen men and women who have risen to a certain level of success in business, sports, entertainment, politics, and even religion, then fall from prominent positions due to character flaws. Character is most often revealed in a successful person when there are strong temptations involving money, power, or sex.

> Success is not achieved by accident. You chart your course by developing good character and good communication skills. —Anna Kendall

Healthy character will ultimately take you further than education, talent, ambition, skills, and experience. It's been said that we will all either become a person of character...or become a character.

Character is about more than just doing the right thing. It's about developing the kind of heart and mind-set that empowers us to survive a crisis intact.

HOW DO YOU BUILD CHARACTER?

1. **Be Sincerely Honest with Yourself.** Of all the lies we tell, the ones we tell ourselves are the most damaging. Question your own motives and stop *justifying* what you know may be wrong, or at least in a gray area. Stop excusing yourself.

2. **Seek Wise Counsel.** We all have blind spots. It's one thing to be honest with yourself, but sometimes we can be blind to our own faults, which are obvious to others. Find two or three people you respect, trust, and believe in. It may not be easy, but ask them for honest and frank feedback regarding how they see you and your life. Maybe they want to jot their thoughts down in writing rather than talking to you face-to-face. They may tell you things about yourself that are unpleasant, but it's valuable information. Use it to learn and grow.

3. **Don't Seek Popularity.** Doing the right thing is almost never easy and may not be popular. It's not a matter of believing you are always right and everyone else is wrong; it simply means you are going to live with a long-range view of what to do, enduring short-term pain for long-term gain. The mature person of character has the ability to postpone immediate gratification for future benefits.

4. **Be Appropriately Transparent.** We'd all like to be something we're not. Be willing to admit your short-comings. You don't have to tell everyone what you're "struggling" with, but you need to tell someone you know and trust. Part of being honest with yourself is being honest with others. And as much as you might be afraid that everyone will think less of you, living transparently and not pretending to be someone you aren't actually makes people think more of you.

5. **Study the Lives of People of Character.** Learn from their lives and experiences. These individuals can make us want to improve, emulate them, and leave a lasting heritage to future generations. If we study the lives of successful men and women from past ages, we find their success came largely from a deeply rooted positive character that was consistently taught in schools, churches, and homes. Character and integrity were seen as the basic foundation of a successful person. Humility, modesty, justice, courage, patience, honesty, and kindness were character qualities that, in the past, were the basic principles of effective and successful living.

6. **Study Character Qualities.**　Discover your Kendall Life Languages Profile and concentrate on strengthening each quality. It's also effective if an entire department or family can work on this together in a *fun* way. For example, you might need to work on punctuality, organization, or diligence. Ask others to help you improve in these areas while you help them in areas that they would like to strengthen. Everyone will grow—a true win-win situation.

7. **Applaud the Character You See in Others**. It reinforces character in you and them. Be a "character-finder," not a "fault-finder."

Character is often revealed in little ways. For example, if a time sheet includes non-billable hours for a particular client, a person of character will bring that to someone's attention.

A person who should be taking responsibility for a mistake but *deliberately* doesn't speak up—and knowingly causes harm or blame to be shifted to another—has a serious character flaw.

> The best index of a person's character is how he treats people who can't do him any good...or how he treats people who can't or won't fight back.
> —advice columnist Abigail Van Buren

Unfortunately, many people do not really know what good character qualities are, how to obtain them, or how to overcome negative character traits. Character development is a daily and life-long growing process. It is intentional and deliberate and can take as much effort as working to build muscles or lose weight.

No matter what your product or service is, you are in the people business. If you invest in your people, you will have a greater chance of leading in your market over other companies who don't. Our system of *Communication IQ* includes the way and means to grow your company to have a culture of character and respect for each other, your customers, and your suppliers.

THE BEST RECOGNITION

The most effective recognition is when we acknowledge character and not accomplishments, whether praising employees, friends, children, or anyone else. When a task is completed well, praise their diligence or their attention to detail, their follow-through, and their creativity.

A true compliment is deep and sincere. Rather than complimenting the task, compliment the character quality that completed the task. For instance, you could say, "It's amazing how you're always able to come up with the right solutions— and because of your diligence, the project was finished before the deadline, too! I'm so glad you're in our department." Or you might tell someone, "Your perseverance is really appreciated." That's much more personal than simply saying, "Good job."

CHARACTER-BASED COMMUNICATION

As a person of character, you want to be a good communicator. Language is not just words. To a deaf person, language is sight and hand signals that speak through the silence. To a blind person, language is the sound that illuminates the loneliness of darkness. To Helen Keller, who was both blind and deaf, language was the caring touch of her teacher, Anne Sullivan.

To a friend, coworker, or employee, language can be a kind word, a pat on the back, or a pleasant, reassuring acknowledgment that the "message" was received.

Around the world, language is a full spectrum of communication elements, a combination of sounds, sights, tastes, smells, touch, writings, drawings, time, light, space, feelings, thoughts, and actions. And it doesn't stop there! Communication includes behavioral patterns, body postures and movement, and unspoken-but-meaningful glances—or glares.

> Through languages, with all their facets, we can either live in peace with our fellow human beings or go to war to try to solve our differences. We can sing joyful songs together and in harmony or we can shout insults in anger at each other. We can experience connection or the pain of being disconnected. We can work together in peace or in pain. The choice is ours. —Anna Kendall

Words are one of the bridges that connect us to other languages. Behavior is another. As you communicate with others, you hear words and observe behaviors that can help you understand the Life Languages they are speaking in that moment as well as your own communication style.

+ Your KLLP reveals your communication profile

+ Your profile reveals your character qualities

+ Your character qualities reveal your passions

+ Your passions reveal your interests, leading to your purpose

✦   Your purpose reveals your effectiveness and your area
    for success

We want you to be the very best *YOU* can be. Your positive, productive communication skills from the Life Languages
program will attract others to you. Negative, non-productive
communication will either push people away or attract unhealthy, negative, or toxic people.

You will be remembered more for your character than for
your accomplishments.

We'd like to share the character goals of an acquaintance
of ours, a professional man in his mid-thirties who writes for
an international television network:

I desire:
1. To become a greater man than I am
2. To encourage joy in others' lives
3. For my word to be more valuable than my sig-
    nature
4. To be sunlight that causes greatness to bloom in
    the lives of others
5. To be and be known as a man of faith, commit-
    ment, and action
6. To make others feel noticed and valued
7. To live a life that inspires, challenges, and en-
    courages others
8. To be a compass that points to "true north"
9. To be a man of talent, accomplishment, courage,
    and perseverance
10. To live a life of destiny fulfilled

11. To impact lives even after I'm gone

12. To dare to be everything God created me to be

Perhaps we should each set goals not to be known or re-membered for our accomplishments, but for our character.

13

DO'S AND DON'TS

W e don't want anyone to misunderstand or possibly misuse the 7 Life Languages. Our years of research and development have been spent with the end goal of making this world a better place by inspiring positive character and effective communication.

In their pure form, each Life Language is unique and can stand alone on the merits of its own character qualities and strengths. The measure and characteristics of success are not limited to any particular Life Language. Each one can be successful in connection or concert with the others. No Life Language is better or worse than any other—all are excellent, unique, dynamic, and filled with greatness. Most importantly, no one is limited or defined by their Kendall Life Languages Profile results. The only boundaries we have are our skills, talents, education, and willingness to work for our passions or vocations.

DO'S AND DON'TS FOR THE LIFE LANGUAGE ASSSESSMENT AND KLLP	
DO's	**DON'Ts**
Accept your languages as unique and special	Compare your languages to others and feel better or worse
Accept others' languages as special to them	Try to change others to only speak your languages
Recognize each language is just as valid as another	Criticize the characteristics of others' languages
Learn to communicate with all languages	Insist others learn your languages instead of learning theirs
Help others learn how to communicate with you	Limit yourself by labeling yourself or others
Enjoy each person's similarities and differences	Give up on learning others' communication preferences
Work on strengthening your weaker languages	Boast or excuse yourself because of your primary language
Choose character	Be a character

Never use your primary Life Language as a label or an excuse. Don't say, "Well, I can't be in charge—I'm just a Responder" or "Don't expect me to be sympathetic. I'm a Doer." You are not a single Life Language, but a complex individual who may have a strong preference for communicating in a certain way.

Everyone speaks all 7 Life Languages at different levels and combinations. Even when a language may be our sixth or seventh, we can still speak it every day or when it helps us communicate or connect with someone else. The Life Languages are not meant to label or limit you. They are intended to *liberate* you.

VIVE LA DIFFÉRENCE

Dealing with people who are different from us can be frustrating...if we choose to be frustrated. Now that you've learned about the 7 Life Languages, however, you have the opportunity to enjoy the unique ways others express themselves and communicate.

IF THERE'S A PARTY AND ALL 7 LIFE LANGUAGES ARE REPRESENTED...

+ **A Responder** hosts the party and spends time with everyone, one at a time, freely giving hugs or pats on the back and offering a caring, listening ear.

+ **A Doer**, the first guest to arrive, immediately starts doing all of the practical things to help out, such as mixing and serving drinks, refilling snack trays and chip bowls, and picking up used plates.

+ **An Influencer** arrives late and leaves last, talking to everyone, telling jokes, and saying goodbye several times before actually leaving.

+ **A Mover** arrives late and wants to leave early unless there are activities, so the Mover may get everyone involved in a game of charades, "Who Am I?" or "Freeze Dance."

+ **A Producer** arrives on time, with an appropriate gift, and leaves on time after organizing an outing to an upcoming special event.

+ **A Shaper** arrives on time, probably without a gift, and leaves on time after talking to everyone about their work and vacation plans.

+ If **a Contemplator** does come, he or she may wander into the library or garden, or sit quietly to one side, away from the crowd, answering questions with humor and wit, or talking with a great deal of passion and insight on a subject the Contemplator is interested in.

APPENDIX:

IN-DEPTH CHARACTERISTICS OF ALL 7 LIFE LANGUAGES

LIFE LANGUAGES
INTERNATIONAL™

APPENDIX A

IN-DEPTH CHARACTERISTICS
OF MOVERS

Courageous	Risk taker	Innovator
Bold	Likes excitement	Forward thinking
High standards	Decisive	Entrepreneurial
Tenacious	Visionary	Change maker
High energy	Results-oriented	Direct
Hyper-vigilant	Proactive	Persuasive
Strong personality	Pioneering	Verbal
Honest	Introspective	Sensitive
Truthful	Assertive	Creative ideas
Perceiver	Dramatic	Introspective

COURAGEOUS, BOLD, TENACIOUS

The Mover language, in its pure form, seems to have natural boldness and courage as part of their character. They like to step up and take on challenges, especially those that are new, different, and require creativity. They will speak up or speak out in meetings because they have the courage to address difficult situations or difficult people head-on. If they are in a situation where there is a conflict or a highly confrontational issue, Movers won't back off from it. They are willing to confront the problem assertively, courageously, fairly, and honestly.

Movers will work well under authority and they expect others to do so as well. If they are in a situation or environment where there is no authority, they will step up and quite naturally fill the gap.

If Movers are doing something important, they become tenacious. When it comes to delivering on an assignment, they will push as hard as necessary to ensure it's completed on time. Making things happen is part of a Mover's DNA.

RISK-TAKER, VISIONARY, INNOVATOR

Movers seize opportunity. They are not frightened by something new. While others may sit back, waiting for a sure thing, Movers will take risks and turn a "marginal business opportunity" into a financial success.

In their mind's eye, they can clearly see the vision and the end result or final goal. And they are usually good at articulating the vision so others will follow and participate. This is important because somewhere between the vision, the innovation, and the end result, Movers often need help to clarify the action steps needed to reach the goal. Finite details are not their strong suit.

Movers like the excitement of a challenge and their risk-taking, adventurous communication style adds to this. They are often described as bundles of energy because they seem capable of anything. They are often doing several things at once, seemingly in constant motion. When they sleep, it's not to rest but to recharge their batteries for the next day's activities. Their minds are continuously in motion, seeking creative and better ways of doing things.

Their high energy also supports their vigilance. They are keenly aware of their surroundings and recognize danger or suspicious activity long before it happens.

Movers can be loved or disliked, but they will rarely be ignored or overlooked. Whatever they do is done with boundless energy and forceful resolve. Strong love, strong opinions, strong results, strong action—eight words that best express the makeup and character of a Mover!

CREATIVE IDEAS

Movers have the talent for always thinking outside the box. They're never at a loss for new ideas, new methods, and new procedures. And because they are so creative with their thinking, in most cases, their new ideas are much better than the old or outdated ones being used.

They are seldom satisfied with the status quo. As far as a Mover is concerned, there is always room for improvement and new ideas.

RESULTS-ORIENTED, PROACTIVE

Movers can talk and listen to ideas only to a point. Then they may become frustrated. They want meetings to produce action steps that generate results as soon as they're implemented. Boredom will cause a Mover to quickly end a committee meeting that appears to be going in circles. To a Mover, all talk and no action is a waste of time.

DIRECT, HONEST, TRUTHFUL

Movers say what they think and are sometimes not be as diplomatic or tactful as one would want. They are direct, truthful, and to the point, so they don't want to hear a story that requires a great build-up. Capture their interest by telling them the bottom line, then say, "Now let me tell you how it happened."

Generally, there is no phoniness about a Mover's speech. They are seldom good at lying or exaggerating the truth. Their eyes, speech, and body language reveal their honest feelings. Movers may have trouble playing poker because their facial expressions and body language give them away.

DECISIVE, PERSUASIVE, VERBAL

Being able to make decisions is an excellent trait. Being able to make correct decisions is even better. Movers are able to make correct decisions rapidly and decisively.

But if the decision turns out to be wrong, Movers pick themselves up and try something better or something new. Regardless, they never lose their ability to be decisive.

Movers are good at speaking spontaneously or impromptu. They often make great sales people as they can sell the vision, idea, or product, and are not afraid to "go for the close." They can almost always motivate others toward a decision.

HIGH STANDARDS, PERCEPTIVE

Movers make major decisions based on their convictions, not on feelings, logic, or circumstances. Their inner convictions and standards are their guiding lights. They believe aiming for high standards helps people live up to their potential and become all that they can be.

By nature, Movers are flexible with working out solutions, but they are uncompromising when it involves their core beliefs.

Their high standards and strong convictions give them a keen awareness of right and wrong. And they have the ability to accurately perceive the motives, character, and reasons for others' actions.

INTROSPECTIVE

As a rule, Movers are very bold and direct, yet they tend to search their hearts and minds to discover if they are operating from an honest and truthful perspective. They are quick to admit when they are wrong or have made a mistake—it's part of their courageous nature. Movers have no problem apologizing when they make a mistake and without fail, they willingly take responsibility for a bad decision.

ASSERTIVE, DRAMATIC

Movers stand up for their beliefs and the rights of others. They express their opinions openly. Assertiveness is a positive characteristic unless the pendulum swings too far and the person becomes overly aggressive.

Many of the positive characteristics of Movers make them seem overly dramatic. They may say shocking things to get your attention. At times, they may do something out of the ordinary to make a point. This is a result of their risk-taking, courage, and innovative characteristics. This dramatic tendency also makes them memorable leaders, speakers, sales people, and teachers.

SENSITIVE

Movers are bold and direct people who make things happen, but they have a sensitive side. It may seem like peeling back the layers on an onion when you look for a Mover's warm, fuzzy side, but once you do get to know them, you find they develop deep and long relationships with many individuals from all walks of life.

Movers often express their sensitivity with boldness and sometimes even tears. Although it's not often openly displayed, Movers have big hearts and they want to help or rescue others. They are concerned, caring people and if they see others going down the wrong path or making unhealthy decisions that can sabotage their lives or future, Movers make a point to intercede.

Note of caution to those who speak the Mover Life Language as their preferred communication style: Movers can move so rapidly that they may not take time to be courteous. Inadvertently, they may fail to use thoughtful words like *thank you* and *please*. Movers can work at making the time to be courteous; those working with Movers can choose to not be offended or feel slighted.

NOTES

APPENDIX B

IN-DEPTH CHARACTERISTICS OF DOERS

Attentive	Detail-oriented	Enjoy serving others
Dependable	Loyal	Have difficulty saying "no"
Diligent	Finisher	Sees immediate needs
Obedient	Enjoys receptive tasks	Likes routine
Organized	High energy	"Now" oriented
Punctual	Good maintainer	Hands-on
Trustworthy	Helpful	Stay busy
Make fast decisions	Work well behind the scenes	Makes lists
Like short-range goals	Observant	Seldom depressed

ATTENTIVE, DETAIL-ORIENTED, DILIGENT

In its pure form, the Doer Life Language pays great attention to details. If you shop with a Doer, you'll observe that they notice any small defect in an item you might be thinking about purchasing. The other languages may not even notice the defect or spend the time checking the item. Doers are also very attentive to practical needs around them.

While some other communication styles see the beginning and the end, Doers see all the necessary steps in between. While others might be inclined to skip over some details, thinking they are unnecessary, Doers know that you reach success by taking care of each step as you come to it.

Meticulous in their organizational ability, they often use color coding or labeling for almost everything in a project. Doers tend to be orderly and organized in their own offices, homes, or other personal spaces. They don't understand how others can function in clutter or disorderliness.

Since the Doer's desire is "to finish," they rarely leave work or an activity until they have finished what they started. Diligence is one of their outstanding characteristics.

DEPENDABLE, LOYAL

When a Doer says they will take care of something, it almost takes an act of Congress for them not to complete the task once it's started. The higher the healthy Doer scores, the more dependable they will be in most areas of practical action.

Doers are generally loyal to those they serve or can help. When they are no longer needed, their loyalty will still be

there, but their effort will be directed to others whose immediate and practical needs they can meet.

SEE IMMEDIATE NEEDS

Doers show their care and concern for people by providing practical service. They are generally not good at meeting emotional needs; for instance, they are not prone to sitting by someone's hospital bed, holding their hand, and comforting them. But without hesitation, Doers offer to do things to help out. They will run errands, mow the lawn for a neighbor, or pick a coworker up to give them a ride to work. Doers make themselves available to meet others' practical need.

HAVE DIFFICULTY SAYING 'NO'

Because Doers are so good at doing most things, many people ask for their assistance. They are often sought-after to coach Little League, speak at Rotary meetings, join a committee, and otherwise pitch in to help. Doers can overextend themselves and burn out if they do not guard against committing to doing too much. For Doers, learning when to say "no" is just as important as knowing when to say "yes."

SELDOM DEPRESSED

When someone is depressed, a great way to help them is to encourage them to get out of bed or off the couch and just doing something. Due to their practical nature, when a Doer feels down, they usually get up, pull out their to-do list, and get back to work.

PUNCTUAL

Being on time is an important part of the Doer's life. They are easily frustrated with people who are chronically late for meetings and lunch dates. They seem to have an internal clock that keeps them on track and punctual.

MAKE FAST DECISIONS

Because they see the practical and pragmatic method of doing things, Doers can make rather rapid decisions. Much of the time, they are spot on; occasionally, however, they need to gather more facts before starting the action.

SHORT-RANGE GOALS; "NOW" ORIENTED

Since the Doer's passion is to finish, it is important for them to have short-range goals that they can start and finish in a day, a week, or some definable date they can manage. Long-range goals must be broken down into "bite size" pieces.

Doers operate in the present moment and like to meet the needs of "now" rather than making plans too far into the future.

ENJOY REPETITIVE TASKS, LIKE ROUTINE

Doers are good with hands-on projects or activities. They are quite capable of doing repetitive tasks without getting bored or growing tired of them. They understand that they can get better and faster at repetitive tasks, which enables them to do more. They *love* to do things!

Plus, if they have a routine system for accomplishing things that works, they don't question it. The Doer's mind-set is, "If it isn't broke, why fix it?"

HIGH ENERGY, STAY BUSY

Doers are so automatic in their "doing" that they are sometimes unaware of what they're doing or just how much they are doing. For instance, they may pick up trash off the floor,

straighten a wall hanging, or close a cabinet door as they walk by.

They have the energy to multi-task and accomplish a lot. Doers are not busy for the sake of being busy. There's a sense of accomplishment with their "busyness."

GOOD MAINTAINER

Whereas a Mover may start a task, but not finish it before moving on to something else, Doers are always ready to lend a helping hand to maintain a project or finish a task.

WORK FROM LISTS

Some people with other communication styles make lists and then can't find the list, or they may think they can remember all of the items they need to buy or tasks they need to do without a list. Doers love to make a list and check off the items as they are finished. They stay organized and feel a sense of accomplishment when they check off an item on their list.

WORK WELL BEHIND THE SCENES

Doers can be great leaders, but they are also comfortable working behind the scenes or being in a secondary leadership role.

A famous conductor of a great symphony orchestra was asked which instrument he considered the most difficult to play. The conductor pondered the question for a moment, then said, "Second fiddle. I can get plenty of *first* violinists, but finding someone who can play second fiddle and do it with enthusiasm—now, that's a problem. And if we have no second fiddles, we have no harmony!" Doers are usually happy to play second fiddle.

Note of caution to those who speak Doer as their primary Life Language: Be careful that you don't say "yes" to too many invitations to serve on committees, too many practical projects, or too much of *anything.* It's easy to burn out if you're not cautious.

NOTES

APPENDIX C

IN-DEPTH CHARACTERISTICS
OF INFLUENCERS

Relational	Encouraging	Charming
Creative	Future-oriented	Think win-win
Enthusiastic	Logical	Flexible
Positive	Verbal	Joyful
Outgoing	Optimistic	Fun
Seldom depressed	Persuasive	Comfortable
Networker	Accepting	Diplomatic
Make fast decisions	Offer solutions	Has many friends
Innovative	Intuitive	Inclusive

FEEL FIRST, THEN THINK

The Influencer Life Language, in its pure form, has two powerhouse strengths that make it particularly invaluable to any organization. With their feeling intelligence, an Influencer is often a very creative "people person," while their thinking intelligence gives them the ability to consistently offer intuitive solutions that can astound others.

These two skills give Influencers the reputation as the people to go to for answers and solutions to major issues. Their cognitive thinking skills and emotive/relational sensitivity will truly amaze those around them.

RELATIONAL, NETWORKER

Influencers are generally friendly and connect easily with other people from all walks of life. They seldom meet a stranger who stays a stranger because they make friends easily.

If an Influencer meets someone they like, they'll want to introduce that person to others they like. They are natural-born networkers and people connectors. The sheer joy of connecting with others and creating new friendships or relationships is what it's all about for an Influencer.

CREATIVE, INNOVATIVE

An Influencer is often into art, music, dancing, decorating, gardening, or other creative activities. If they are not personally talented in any of these areas, they usually do have a natural appreciation for the arts. They enjoy artistic creation.

Their creativity also adds to their ability to innovate and seek solutions. If there's a project with problems and the group appears to be stuck, the Influencer may very well be the one to find a solution, often *outside the box*, somewhat like Movers.

ENTHUSIASTIC, OPTIMISTIC, ENCOURAGING

You can generally recognize Influencers because of their positive, upbeat characteristics. Even in the midst of bad news—even a disaster—they will find a silver lining out there somewhere, no matter how many dark clouds appear. This may cause others to think the Influencer is minimizing the problem. However, the Influencer knows there are two options—see the worst or focus on the best. They choose the latter.

SELDOM DEPRESSED

Because Influencers have such a positive attitude toward life and an equally optimistic world view, they are seldom depressed. When or if they ever feel down, that behavior or mood usually doesn't last long.

For the Influencer, being depressed is just plain boring. Should they happen to feel depressed or moody, they will take action to get back into a positive mind-set again, such as going out and meeting someone for coffee or catching a movie. They get up, get out, and get going!

THINK WIN-WIN

Influencers want everyone to win. If they are working on a project, solution, contract, or anything else that involves others, they instinctually want it to be good and fair for everyone. They don't want anyone to lose or be left out.

INCLUSIVE, ACCEPTING

Even as little children, those who score high in the Influencer Life Language want to include everyone in the game. They don't like for others to feel left out and they almost always carry this positive attitude over into their adult life.

The two-for-lunch date can easily turn into seven or eight people if the Influencer feels they have left someone out. Excluding people from a group is simply not acceptable!

An Influencer accepts others easily and is rarely bothered by another person's differences. Having such a wide, sweeping, positive overview of life and people gives Influencers the ability to comfortably deal with another person's unproductive behavior or negative conduct. They almost always find something good in everyone.

DIPLOMATIC, CHARMING, TACTFUL

Influencers seem to know the right words to say at the right time. If they are unexpectedly called upon to speak to a group, they may not have any idea what they are going to say in that impromptu moment. Regardless, they seem rise to the occasion—and when they speak, it usually sounds like they have spent weeks preparing their message.

FUN, OUTGOING, JOYFUL

You can depend on an Influencer to have a great sense of humor. They want people they're with to have fun and enjoy themselves. Most people like to be around Influencers because of their ability to easily build relationships and make others feel comfortable.

FLEXIBLE, MAKE FAST DECISIONS

If a project is not working and the Influencer realizes the direction they are taking is not good or even wrong, they will switch gears and try another option. They are not threatened by change.

Influencers will usually quickly listen to and review opinions, then rapidly weigh the facts and make a decision. Although they prefer to reach a consensus, in the absence of one, they will decide. Their flexibility is easily observable if something isn't right or adjustments are needed. Influencers seldom get stuck.

FUTURE-ORIENTED

Influencers are able to learn from the past and it's in their nature to be forward-thinking and future-oriented. Like Movers, Influencers move forward with life and embrace it, looking forward to what is yet to come.

Note of caution to those whose primary Life Language is Influencer: Not wanting to disappoint anyone or cause someone to feel left out, you may tend to overcommit yourself, both socially and professionally. Take steps to ensure this doesn't happen. Taking on too much can eventually cause anyone to burn out, regardless of their preferred communication style.

NOTES

APPENDIX D

IN-DEPTH CHARACTERISTICS OF RESPONDERS

Accepting	Verbal	Second Language visible
Relational	Available	Easily shakes hands or hugs
Reaches out	Compassionate	Protective
Physically responsive	Many friends, but few close	Likes to please
Peacekeeper	Creative	Humility
Athletic	Sensitive	Prefers friends one-on-one
Gentle	Enjoys contact sports	Supports underdog
"Now" oriented	Likes approval	Loyal
Sincere	Emotional energy	Carries burdens

SECOND LANGUAGE VISIBLE

Those whose primary communication style is Responder are often transparent in that their second Life Language can freely come "forward" to be seen and heard first. Although Responder is definitely their first Life Language, the second communication style is usually obvious.

LIKE APPROVAL

In its pure form, the Responder Life Language has a deep-seated need to be accepted and approved. Because of this innate trait, many Responders prefer to get consensus prior to making a final, major decision.

"NOW" ORIENTED

Responders tend to live in the present moment, appreciate it, and enjoy it. Being fully present and living in the "now" moment, Responders can be sensitive to the needs of others.

ACCEPTING, RELATIONAL

Responders tend to accept people just as they are and generally never seek to change them or look for their weaknesses. They also seldom try to change unacceptable traits or habits of others. Acceptance is part of their positive character and way of life.

Relationships are very important to Responders. They make people around them feel welcome. Responders generally have many acquaintances, but they are selective when it comes to choosing their close friends.

REACH OUT, COMPASSIONATE, PASSIONATE

Responders want to help individuals who are hurting. They have a desire to help make other people's issues, pain, and problems go away. They will take the time to listen and they do want to hear what's in the minds and hearts of others. Responders often protect, defend, and assist the underdog or people they feel have been treated unfairly or unjustly.

Responders are compassionate toward others and passionate about things they believe in. They are known for putting passion into everything they do in their life and relationships. They are drawn to jobs, causes, or missions that they truly feel passionate about and sincerely believe in.

PROTECTIVE, LOYAL

Responders are protective of those they care about and want to see that others who are in lesser positions, both professionally and personally, are also equally protected.

Responders are loyal and protective of their friends, family, team members, and their departments, whether they are supervisors and employees. Exhibiting a protective nature is not an unusual leadership trait for a Responder. Responders want and expect to be secure in the knowledge that they and others are being treated fairly.

GENTLE BUT STRONG

It takes a lot of strength to be gentle. Anyone can be a bully, which is a sign of weakness. To be able to be strong enough to be a good leader, while having a gentle and knowing touch, is an innate ability of the Responder Life Language.

HUMBLE

Healthy Responders tend to be humble. They will give the team or group they oversee as much praise as they get. They "pass it on."

SENSITIVE, VULNERABLE

Responders are personally sensitive and can be easily hurt, but they are also sensitive to other people's hurts. It is important for Responders to guard their own hearts. They can listen and show concern, but must be careful to not inadvertently take on another's need and make it their own.

Because Responders care and feel so deeply, they can also be hurt more deeply than many of the other Life Languages. They are the most vulnerable to emotional pain because their hearts are almost always open to others.

SINCERE, AVAILABLE

When Responders show compassion or humility, they do so with great sincerity. It comes from their heart and mind because they feel deeply.

Responders let their friends, family, and coworkers know they are available or when they will be. Sometimes, the act of being available is a great blessing to others. It can also become an issue for a Responder because they tend to put the needs of others ahead of their own needs and prior commitments or plans.

RESPONSIVE, LIKE TO PLEASE

Responders are generally very verbally expressive. They also like to respond physically in a conversation with gestures of agreement or disagreement about a particular subject, nodding or shaking their head. In a group, they like to please others and keep the peace. They often try to keep conflict out of their workplace or home, operating as a peacekeeper.

Of the 7 Life Languages, Responders tend to demonstrate the most love. People who speak the other communication styles actually love just as much, but Responders do so more openly and freely.

SHAKE HANDS, GIVE HUGS

Responders are usually physically affirming of others, showing their warmth and concern with a hug, a pat on the back, or another display of affection. They need to be cautious when moving too close into someone else's personal space because such physical gestures could be misinterpreted.

CREATIVE

Responders, like Influencers, tend to be musical, artistic, and creative. They may enjoy cooking, gardening, or decorating, and have an appreciation for the arts.

ATHLETIC, HAVE EMOTIONAL ENERGY

Responders often participate in contact sports. This surprises many who see Responders as creative, sensitive individuals. But it takes energy to compete in sports and their emotions could be described as *energy in motion*. A Responder employee will usually work tirelessly for their team or department.

Note of caution to those whose primary Life Language is Responder: Because of your sensitivity, you must try not to internalize or take on the pain or issues of other people. Don't get depressed when they share their burdens with you. Protect your own feelings.

NOTES

APPENDIX E

IN-DEPTH CHARACTERISTICS
OF SHAPERS

Organized and efficient	Enjoys planning	Pursues excellence
Sets long-range goals	Endurance	Visionary
Responsible	Natural born leader	Tolerant
Delegator	Future-oriented	Develops others
Successful	Communicates ideas, plans	Looks for results
Single-minded and focused	Learns from past	Decisive
Uses charts, graphs, lists	Discreet	Values appearance
Expects preparedness	Time-sensitive	Dislikes most small talk
Watches bottom line	Embraces change	Could be workaholic

ORGANIZED, EFFICIENT PLANNER

In its pure form, the Shaper Life Language always stays involved with any project or company goal, from inception, through the execution, and until its ultimate conclusion. In some cases, Shapers will continue their involvement with a project and, if necessary, provide appropriate follow-ups or adjustments to the delivered product or plan.

The ability to create long-range plans is a skill that many Shapers develop at a young age. It's not unusual for a young Shaper in junior high school to already know exactly what they want to do after high school. Their long-range plans may include where they want to go to college or even graduate school.

Shapers are ambitious about knowing what they want and how to successfully plan to get it. Setting more long-range, future goals that can be years off are part of their mental thought process and how they routinely think.

Shapers also demonstrate endurance. They're in the game for the long haul. Shapers have patience for their plans.

VISIONARY

Like Movers, Shapers are visionary. When a Shaper is organizing or producing something, they have the ability to see the needed steps of action from A to Z, from the beginning to the end. This visionary skill is further supported by their ability to plan and set goals, both short-term and long-range.

NATURAL BORN LEADER

Shapers often don't even try to move into a position of leadership. Their gifts seem to get them moved, and sometimes shoved, into a lead role. Sometimes, a leadership position may even be created for them. They naturally rise to the occasion and when they do, they are generally mentally and emotionally well-prepared to handle it.

DELEGATE, DEVELOP OTHERS

Shapers naturally delegate parts of an assignment to other people. Then they carefully manage and supervise to make sure all elements of the job are being done correctly. After delegating work assignments, they continue to check the job's progress until it's completed.

Shapers are usually good at developing others. When they delegate a portion of an assignment to a coworker and are impressed with the results, it's not unusual for them to step in and help to develop that person to move up in their career and life.

SINGLE-MINDED, FOCUSED

Shapers stay focused on the goal of delivering a quality product on time. They deal with any personal or professional needs, activities, or problems that arise in a scheduled, prioritized manner. The Shaper's primary mind-set is to stay focused on the goals of the plan and remain unwavering during the process.

DECISIVE, DISCREET

Shapers don't spend a lot of time second guessing their decisions. If a decision turns out to be wrong, they'll make the needed corrections and change or adjust course. Before they "pull the plug" on any project, they will carefully weigh all of the facts to see what can be used in another area.

You can depend on a Shaper to be discrete. They seem to understand intuitively what needs to be held close to the chest and kept private and what needs to be shared with others.

EXPECT ORDERLINESS, EXCELLENCE

Shapers are generally well-prepared and they expect others to share this trait. If you have a planned meeting with a Shaper, take your ideas, facts, paperwork, charts, and graphs—your due diligence to support your ideas—and present your case in a direct, organized, and orderly fashion. Shapers want to know that the work you're about to present represents serious thought and effort, that it's not some spur-of-the-moment idea.

Shapers pursue excellence in their work and home and appreciate others who do the same.

Shapers don't usually believe in change without facts and research to back up a plan to justify a major change. If your plan isn't well thought out and documented with facts, it's not likely to impress a Shaper. But, if your plan has merit and you're convinced it will bring about success and improvement to the organization, rest assured, a Shaper will be ready and willing to get behind it.

WATCH BOTTOM LINE

Shapers have an awareness of return on investment and watching the bottom line. They know what it takes to make a business successful and keep it that way.

RESPONSIBLE, TOLERANT

Shapers understand responsibility and are not afraid of the demands that leadership requires. Honoring commitments are part of a Shaper's DNA.

Interestingly, Shapers will tolerate someone they may not especially like if that person can do the job and move the plan forward.

FUTURE-ORIENTED

Shapers embrace the future and if not careful, they can tend to neglect the present. However, this is how they accomplish so much: by seeing how to create plans that are far-reaching, with built-in controls and guidelines that will not only help the company's day-to-day success, but also its future success.

LEARN FROM THE PAST

Shapers are generally very good at studying and learning from past successes and failures, and using this knowledge and experience to build toward a greater future.

SUCCESSFUL, VALUE "APPEARANCES"

Shapers are so success-oriented that they usually accept nothing less than first place. All their plans and focus are directed toward producing excellence and success. Shapers look for and expect results.

Shapers generally understand the concept of dressing for success. They believe that part of being successful is looking successful and wearing appropriate clothing.

SENSITIVE TO TIME

Shapers seem to realize that *time is money* and therefore, they don't like to waste it. If you are in working relationship with a Shaper, be aware of how Shapers feel about time and how to use it appropriately.

Note of caution to those with Shaper as their primary Life Language: Be aware of the tendency to become a workaholic. Because of your continuing pursuit of excellence, your keen ability to focus, and your desire, almost at all costs, to succeed, you could easy lose sight and even forget about the needs of your family and your own personal health.

NOTES

APPENDIX F

IN-DEPTH CHARACTERISTICS
OF PRODUCERS

Well-rounded individuals	Responsible	Strive for excellence
Sufficient	Good with action	Hospitable
Abundance	Gracious	Often good communicators
Give thoughtful gifts	Welcoming	Cognitively generous
Emotively graceful	Balanced	Prepared with resources
Courteous	Good money managers	Micro-manager
Thrifty	Looks for quality	Looks for savings
Resourceful	Good people skills	Exhibits vitality

WELL-ROUNDED, BALANCED

The Producer Life Language, in its pure form, appears to consistently be the most well-rounded of all the communication styles. The Producer character qualities seem to overlap one another, supporting the each other and making them all stronger.

Producers are in the cognitive intelligence category, but it's not unusual for them to lean to the kinetic/action or emotive/feeling intelligence languages. Producers can seem to be emotive and yet they can put action to what they need. In a sense, then, Producers can cover all three intelligence categories. They are very capable and relatable.

Because of their natural tendency to be proper and professional, Producers are usually tactful and diplomatic. This is part of their well-roundedness.

MAKE DECISIONS EASILY

After considering facts and situations, Producers make decisions easily. They tend to possess great wisdom and intuition.

SUFFICIENCY, ABUNDANCE

No matter what their income, Producers seem to function from a position of sufficiency and often abundance. They do research, seek, compare, and find the best buys, the best bargains, and the highest quality items, usually at exceptional prices.

GIVE THOUGHTFUL GIFTS

Producers seem to learn and remember what a person likes or prefers. They buy and give quality gifts—not necessarily the most expensive gifts, but the *most appropriate*. Producers also put away gifts (in a special place) that will be appropriate for many people, so gifts are there, waiting for the right moment to be given. This is part of the Producer's ability to be thoughtful and generous. Producers are also thoughtful with thank-you notes and cards.

They are basically philanthropic, but do not give to every need or every homeless person who solicits help. Instead, Producers study the need or situation first. Then they may wait and give a significant gift to a cause they feel shows good management and proper use of their funds.

GOOD WITH MONEY, RESOURCES

To the amazement of most people who know them, Producers seem to be prepared for any and all situations. To this Life Language, preparedness is a natural and expected way to live and do business.

Producers are naturally gifted in handling money and resources. They often earn significant income in their lifetimes and generally retire with financial security and dignity. Even if they do not acquire great wealth, they generally use their money wisely and efficiently.

They are resourceful, with finding the best ways to use items, money, and situations. Producers are always looking for savings and bargains. Because they are careful about how they spend money, both at work and at home, they have no problem looking for quality items that have lasting value. Producers like to give direction about where the money goes, rather than tracking where it has been.

HOSPITABLE, SELDOM DEPRESSED

If a Producer knows you are coming to their home or office, they welcome you with open arms, making you feel as if they have been preparing for your visit for weeks, not minutes. Even if you pay them a surprise visit, you will not catch them off-guard and they'll be happy to see you, ready to offer refreshments and make sure you are comfortable.

The psychiatrist Dr. Karl Menninger once said, "People who are generous and grateful are seldom if ever depressed." Producers are both generous and grateful, so depression is rarely a part of their life.

GOOD AT MANAGING PEOPLE

Because Producers are so gracious, hospitable, and welcoming, they are naturals at making others feel special and valued. People enjoy being in the presence of Producers, so they also tend to be good at managing people. However, they prefer to limit the number of people they are managing, opting for a handful of assistant managers who oversee people under them.

Note of caution to those whose primary Life Language is Producer: Make sure you do not give any gift that has "strings attached." Every gift you give must be given freely, from the heart, expecting nothing in return.

NOTES

APPENDIX G

IN-DEPTH CHARACTERISTICS OF CONTEMPLATORS

Cautious	Complex thinkers	Need alone time
Seek contentment	Quiet	Not easily controlled
Exhibit deference	Private	Deep thinkers
Determined	Have well-defined boundaries	Validate truth
Loyal	Guard their time	Research facts
Visibly unresponsive	Unusual sense of humor	Think before speaking
Dislike change	Verbal when interested	Higher IQ
Not very sensitive	Calm	Avoid conflict
Need private space	Comfortable with silence	Philosophical & studious
Have many interests	Life-long learners	Analytical

CAUTIOUS, DISLIKE CHANGE

In its pure form, the Contemplator Life Language is basically cautious and resistant to change. The Contemplator also tends to move or adjust to new activities somewhat slowly. When they settle into a pattern and become comfortable and content, a Contemplator often sees no need for change, so they initially resist it until or unless they become convinced of the need.

Positive by nature, Contemplators resist change only because in their highly analytical mind, they will think, "Why reinvent the wheel?" or "If it's not broken, don't fix it."

COMPLEX

Because they think so deeply and are so intelligent, Contemplators may seem difficult to communicate with. Mentally accessing all of their thoughts, feelings, and experiences, then sorting all that out, generally causes a Contemplator to speak or answer a question rather slowly. This is not deliberate, but the slow reaction time can cause those who are listening and waiting for a response to easily feel as if the Contemplator is uninterested, unconcerned, or even avoiding the question, as if they don't know the answer. The opposite is generally the truth.

QUIET...OR TALKATIVE

Contemplators is quite comfortable with silence or a quiet atmosphere. Other Life Languages seem to want to fill the silence with talk, television, music, or something else. However, when Contemplators talk about something they are interested in or passionate about, they may *talk and talk*, giving you far more information than you'll ever need. They are usually very verbal when discussing a topic of interest to them.

PHILOSOPHICAL, MANY INTERESTS

Contemplators understand many theories and the depth of their knowledge and wisdom can be overwhelming. This can make for some very deep discussions, filled with many different sides and points of view about any subject. Contemplators can be extremely informative and, on occasion, very entertaining, offering the unsuspecting listener a wonderful and provocative learning experience.

Many Contemplators have so many interests that it may be hard for them to settle down into a solid career path. But once they do, they have what it takes to soar to success. Contemplators are often gifted in music or writing and may speak multiple cultural languages.

PRIVATE, NEED PRIVATE SPACE

Often, Contemplator men have facial hair, which may be indicative of their desire for privacy as well as doing their own thing. Only those who take the time to really get to know a Contemplator coworker or friend will know what goes on inside their mind. A Contemplator is not naturally inclined to freely share their deep, complex feelings and thoughts with others.

Occasionally, they need their own space. Generally, they are not comfortable with acquaintances, coworkers, or even those close to them invading their space too often. It's better to let the Contemplator invite you into their office than to just go in and sit down.

AVOID CONFLICT, LOVE PEACE

Like everyone else, Contemplators can max out and reach their top level of annoyance, frustration, or anger. For the most part, Contemplators try to avoid conflict and may just walk away from it. Living or working in an environment that is filled with conflict is detrimental to their peace and mental health. Those with Contemplator as their primary Life Language are not necessarily peacekeepers, but they strongly desire personal peace and may leave a situation to get it.

PERSONALLY SENSITIVE

Contemplators are not especially attuned to how their personal actions and idiosyncrasies might offend or confuse others, but they are wired to being personally sensitive. They can quickly internalize slights, hurts, offenses, and insensitive gestures made toward them.

You may hurt a Contemplator's feelings and not even know it because their facial expression would not show it. They may hold on to a particular upsetting issue for days or months, then one day tell you something is bothering them regarding something you said or did. If you realize that you have just hurt or offended a Contemplator, address it immediately and try to correct the situation.

SET BOUNDARIES, GUARD THEIR TIME

Contemplators may arrive late or plan to go somewhere and then, at the last minute, get involved with something else and forget to show up. Or they may call you to let you know they're not coming. Contemplators are serious about guarding their own personal time and space. They feel equally serious about having well-defined boundaries.

Not everyone is invited into their space or gets to share in their thoughts and feelings. Although it's normal to feel slighted and upset when a Contemplator doesn't show up for a meeting or personal appointment, we should try not to feel hurt or angry. Contemplators simply march to a different drummer.

NOT EASILY CONTROLLED

Contemplators can make excellent employees and will bring a deep, exceptional performance to any team. They are happy to follow a leader or be the leader of an assignment or task, which they do quite effectively. They are not easily controlled, manipulated, or bullied.

Contemplators are easy to reason with and trust. They will follow the plans or rules of an organization, but they may take a different route getting there. As children and adults, Contemplators are usually not prone to peer pressure or following the "in" crowd.

UNUSUAL SENSE OF HUMOR

Contemplators can be so clever that it may take others a day or two to catch the meaning or punch line of their jokes. At times, Albert Einstein's humor almost seemed to bubble out of him. In a November 1901 letter to his future bride, Mileva Maric, he wrote, "It is very cozy in the new room, even though its only ornaments are myself and the dear red lampshade."

Einstein's May 1905 letter to close friend Conrad Habicht included this pithy complaint:

So, what are you up to, you frozen whale, you smoked, dried, canned piece of soul, or whatever else I would like to hurl at your head, filled as I am with 70% anger and 30% pity! You have only the latter 30% to thank for my not having sent you a can full of minced onions and garlic after you so cravenly did not show up on Easter.

LOYAL

Contemplators are loyal to the past and the present. If someone is ever a friend of theirs, they will generally always consider them to be a real friend, even if they haven't had contact with them in years. Time, distance, or lack of contact does not affect a Contemplator's loyalty or feelings.

STUDIOUS, LIFE-LONG-LEARNERS

Contemplators never seem to tire of learning. This keeps them fresh, current, and usually very knowledgeable about numerous subjects. They get great satisfaction from studying, reasoning, analyzing, and continuing the learning process all of their lives.

Note of caution to those whose primary Life Language is Contemplator: Stay connected with others by initiating discussions with them, sharing your thoughts and discoveries. Look for ways to acknowledge their feelings, too. Make it a two-way relationship.

NOTES

ABOUT THE AUTHORS

Fred and **Anna Kendall** are known nationally and internationally as experts in communication and relationships. They have offered their expert advice as hosts or interview guests on more than eight hundred television and radio programs, including *Dr. Phil* and *Good Morning America*. Their interest in helping people understand themselves and others was the catalyst for creating, developing, and perfecting an original system of communication known as the 7 Life Languages. They also developed the Kendall Life Languages Profile (KLLP), an exceptional measurement instrument that reveals one's fluency in the seven different communication styles. This foundational product is both diagnostic and prescriptive, providing insightful, positive self-discovery resulting in character-centered communication.

Fred's eclectic background includes positions such as juvenile probation counselor and officer, area and divisional manager of electronics communication companies, hospital management, and co-ownership of three psychiatric hospital programs and seventeen outpatient centers called LifeCare, located in Ft. Worth, Texas, Albuquerque, New Mexico, and Newport Beach, California. He has served on advisory councils and boards of directors for several organizations.

Anna was the publicist and personal executive assistant to Mary Kay Ash, founder of Mary Kay Cosmetics, Inc., eventually becoming an international senior director. She co-hosted the nationwide radio talk show, *Point of View*, as well as her own shows, *The Christian Home* and *Love Restores*. Anna also hosted *LifeCare*, a national television talk show on emotional, relational, and professional issues that was syndicated on network and independent stations.

With Fred's education and experience in military science, psychology, psychometrics, and business, combined with Anna's extensive background in public relations, marketing, advertising, and communication, the Kendalls formed Life Languages International in 1995.

For more information, visit www.lifelanguages.com.

BIBLIOGRAPHY

Chapter 4. Example of a Famous Mover, President Theodore "Teddy" Roosevelt

+ *Theodore Roosevelt: An Autobiography* by Theodore Roosevelt (www.gutenberg.org/files/3335/3335-h/3335-h. htm).

+ The Almanac of Theodore Roosevelt (www.theodore-roosevelt.com).

Chapter 5. Example of a Famous Doer, President Jimmy Carter

+ The Nobel Peace Laureate Project, "American Winners of the Nobel Peace Prize" (www.nobelpeacelaureates. org/pdf/Jimmy_Carter.pdf).

+ Kevin Sullivan and Mary Jordan, "The un-celebrity president: Jimmy Carter shuns riches, lives modestly in his Georgia hometown," *The Washington Post*, August 17, 2018 (www.washingtonpost.com/news/national/wp/2018/08/17/feature/the-un-celebrity-president-jimmy-carter-shuns-riches-lives-modestly-in-his-georgia-hometown/?utm_term=.5229ec0ced1c).

+ The National Constitution Center, "10 fascinating facts about former President Jimmy Carter," October 1, 2018 (constitutioncenter.org/blog/10-fascinating-facts-about-former-president-jimmy-carter).

+ The Carter Center (www.cartercenter.org).

+ "Jimmy Carter and the Complexity of Political Motives," excerpts from *New York Times Magazine* article by Jim Wooten, quoted in Jurg Steiner's *Conscience in Politics: An Empirical Investigation of Swiss Decision Cases* (New York: Garland Publishing, Inc., 1996).

+ Jimmy Carter, *Sources of Strength: Meditations on Scripture for a Living Faith* (New York, NY: Three Rivers Press, 1997).

Chapter 6. Example of a Famous Influencer, President Ronald Reagan

+ Dan Rather with Lloyd Vries, "Ronald Reagan, Master Storyteller," *Forty Eight Hours*, *CBS News*, June 7, 2004 (www.cbsnews.com/news/ronald-reagan-master-storyteller).

+ The American Presidency Project, "Ronald Reagan" (www.presidency.ucsb.edu/people/president/ronald-reagan).

+ Ronald Reagan Presidential Foundation and Institute (www.reaganfoundation.org).

+ The Ronald Reagan Presidential Library and Museum (www.reaganlibrary.gov).

Chapter 7. Example of a Famous Responder, Mother Teresa of Calcutta

+ Catholic Link (catholic-link.org/quotes-author/mother-teresa-of-calcutta).

+ Biography Online (www.biographyonline.net/nobelprize/mother_teresa.html).

+ Catholic Online: World's Catholic Library (www.catholic.org/saints/saint.php?saint_id=5611).

+ Hector Welgampola, "Mother Teresa's anger had a subtle message," *Matters India*, August 2016 (mattersindia.com/2016/08/mother-teresas-anger-had-a-subtle-message).

+ Leo Maasburg, *Mother Teresa of Calcutta: A Personal Portrait: 50 Inspiring Stories Never Before Told* (San Francisco: Ignatius Press, 2011).

+ Mother Teresa, *No Greater Love* (Novato, CA: New World Library, 1997).

Chapter 8. Example of a Famous Shaper, General H. Norman Schwarzkopf

- The American Academy of Achievement, "General H. Norman Schwarzkopf, USA" (www.achievement.org/achiever/general-h-norman-schwarzkopf).

- Biography, "Norman Schwarzkopf, General, 1934–2012" (www.biography.com/people/norman-schwarz-kopf-9476401).

- Adam Entous, "General Led International Coalition in First Gulf War," *The Wall Street Journal*, December 27, 2012 (www.wsj.com/articles/ SB10001424127887324 669104578206131116000740).

- Norman Schwarzkopf with Peter Petre, *It Doesn't Take a Hero: The Autobiography of General Norman Schwarz-kopf* (New York: Bantam Books, 1992).

Chapter 9. Example of a Famous Producer, Jacqueline "Jackie" Kennedy Onassis

- The John F. Kennedy Presidential Library and Museum (www.jfklibrary.org).

- Malea Walker, "Jackie Kennedy: Inquiring Camera Girl," The Library of Congress, May 22, 2018 (blogs. loc.gov/headlinesandheroes/2018/05/jackie-kennedy-inquiring-camera-girl).

- Amy Higley, "5 Life Lessons from Jackie Kennedy," Faith Counts, December 19, 2016 (faithcounts. com/5-life-lessons-jackie-kennedy).

+ Evan Andrews, "10 Things You May Not Know About Jacqueline Kennedy Onassis," The History Channel, July 28, 2014 (www.history.com/news/10-things-you-may-not-know-about-jacqueline-kennedy-onassis).

+ Nancy Bilyeau, "Jackie Kennedy's Third Act: How the twice-widowed American icon became a successful book editor—at $200 a week," *Town & Country* magazine, August 18, 2017.

+ The New York Preservation Archive Project (www.nypap. org/preservation-history/jacqueline-kennedy-onassis).

+ The National First Ladies' Library (www.firstladies. org/biographies/firstladies. aspx?biography=36).

Chapter 10. Example of a Famous Contemplator, Albert Einstein

+ Albert Einstein, "Notes for an Autobiography," *The Saturday Review of Literature*, November 26, 1949 (archive.org/details/EinsteinAutobiography/page/n0).

+ *The Collected Papers of Albert Einstein*, Princeton University Press (einsteinpapers.press.princeton.edu).

+ John Archibald Wheeler, *Albert Einstein, 1879 – 1955, a Biographical Memoir* (Washington, D.C.: The National Academy of Sciences, 1980);

+ (www.nasonline.org/publications/biographical-memoirs/memoir-pdfs/einstein-albert.pdf).

+ The American Museum of Natural History, "Profile: Albert Einstein"

+ (www.amnh.org/learn/pd/physical_science/profiles/ aeinstein.html).

TO TAKE THE LIFE LANGUAGES ASSESSMENT, PLEASE VISIT:

HTTPS://WWW.LIFELANGUAGES.COM/PROMO/COMMUNICATIONIQ

OR SCAN THIS CODE:

FOR THE KENDALL LIFE LANGUAGES PROFILE (KLLP), PLEASE VISIT:

WWW.LIFELANGUAGES.COM